I DON'T
WANNA LOSE
MY WIFE!
(WHEN IT'S **TOO LATE** TO SAY I'M **SORRY**.)

BY **RAW**
(THE **CHEAT**OLOGIST)

"WHEN YOU'RE A CHEATER, LIES ARE YOUR LIFE."

CONFESSIONS OF THE HEART

AN OPEN APOLOGY TO ALL THE MOTHERS AND WIVES THAT HAD TO ENDURE THIS PAIN…..AND TO THE MOTHER OF MY CHILDREN, MY FORMER WIFE; TO WHOM I REGRET BETRAYING.

"BROKEN THINGS CAN BECOME BLESSED THINGS IF YOU LET GOD DO THE MENDING …I'M SORRY THAT I HURT YOU."

INTRODUCTION

This book is about me cheating on my wife. It's about the deception, lies and the pain I caused her that inadvertently changed the course of our lives **forever**…Who I was, what I became, and who I am today as a result of cheating.

We were supposed to be happily married, with a big white house, with a picket fence, beautiful children, a dog and a cat. Amazingly, we had this all. But what I can't understand, for the life of me, how did I lose it all just like that….Why did I compromise my dreams fulfilled, to a nightmare waiting? What did I get out of this unfaithfulness? Truthfully, the benefit of my betrayal left me with nothing at all but humiliation, guilt and a sense of unworthiness.

I can honestly relate to the song by the artist Tank, "Maybe I Deserve." His words are now my very own confession: *"Maybe I deserve, for you to go out and find somebody new… maybe I deserve, for you to stay out all night…maybe I deserve, to be lied to sometimes… maybe I deserved it."*

The sad thing is, after being conscious of what I was doing to my marriage, and to my wife, I persisted down a path of disrespect, deception and pain as if I enjoyed hurting and destroying her. How much would she bare before she eventually says "I'm fed up?"

My wife forgave me over and over again. Or did she really have a motive of her own? Was she planning a get back?

Whatever the case may be, I needed to reach a point when I could forgive myself. This would become extremely difficult because I never thought of what I was doing, on the outside, was actually a bad thing. Nor did I think it would become so detrimental to my home life.

Why did I do this? What led me down this rotten path of deceit? I once was a happily married man, a family man, and a good man… then I became a depressed man, void of reasoning and the worst kind of cheater.

What affected my thinking? What reset the moral pace of my heart? What made my spirit condone my frequent penetrations? How could I change my ways? Would I ever change my ways?

This is my story…My drama…My confessions.

<u>From the Author</u>

Here are some things you need to know about me: First of all, I love women. I love to chase women, I love the art of flirtation and I love it when I conquer their womb. I felt I needed to sex other women just as much as I needed oxygen to breathe. No matter how good one experience was, I needed different women to experience.

I was not a sex fein, but I feined to have different woman screaming my name in ecstasy. I loved it when women dug their nails in my back. I loved it when they said "Don't stop, Don't stop!" I loved how they told me how good I licked them, or how good I made them feel when I pounded their bottom out. I lived for their pleasure; even at the expense of sabotaging my own.

I loved to think that I was getting over on my wife too…that she really didn't know I lived this secret life. My mind was twisted and my values horribly misplaced though because I slept with equally, or more, women while I was married than I did before I was married. I just became a little more sensitive to my wife's feelings.

At first, I moved discreetly…I tried to perfect my method of cheating so that it would never hit home. I never wanted to upset and hurt my wife. I never planned to leave my wife. I never intended to love and want another woman, more than my own wife.

"I was just fuckin' them girls; I was gonna get right back…"

Well, that's what Jay Z said, and my wife loved Jay Z and repeated his verse. So why couldn't she believe it when I said it?

Of course, I'm a liar and I'm a cheater. This book is a journey into the heart, mind and soul of a cheating man. I promise you it will be worth the read.....and don't judge me; Just pray for me....and avoid being me.

Prelude

It's amazing, how I have so much to say, so much to write, but don't know where to begin. Should I start with the affair I had with Crystal?

Crystal was a one night stand. I met her on a Sunday, while shopping in Wal-Mart with my wife. I was in the electronics section, and my wife was in the grocery aisle. _That was one of my problems. I always wandered off when I was shopping with my wife, looking for some other women to lust over._ I slipped my number to Crystal that Sunday and was in her guts later that evening. I never called her again.

Maybe I should start with the good part of my life, where we lived together as a family, before I started exploring. I was really a good man...I just couldn't keep my hands to myself, and I couldn't keep my eyes from wandering.

The truth is, no matter how I begin my story I cheated more times than I can remember. It's a shame because after a week, I couldn't remember their names, just the episodes. I kept promising myself that I wouldn't do it again because it was wrong what I was doing to my wife and to our family. But I did it again.

At first, I never confessed my ill-mannered behavior to my wife. I lived a life of deception for a longtime. But she kept snooping for stuff, so she found it.

When my wife started to find phone numbers in my jeans, overheard late night calls and witnessed me staying out all night, she became suspicious. She witnessed a glimpse of my deception and became a detective. She started following me around, popping up unexpectedly at my job; harassing my homeboys and questioning them about my whereabouts (trying to catch me in a lie later.)

She started going in to my cellular phone, reading my text messages, sending messages on my phone just to see who would respond back. She would go through the computer, looking for anything I left behind indicating another woman.

She smelled my clothes for another woman's scent; she even asked to smell my dick sometimes. It became sickening to me. So sickening that I would purposely start fights and arguments just to have a reason to leave and stay out all night. Not all the time to cheat, but just to clear my head.

I would rent a hotel room just to chill and be alone for the moment. However, I couldn't be alone for too long. So of course, I would call another woman to the room and fuck my stress away. The other woman wanted to comfort me by freaking me. That was more licking, sucking and fucking.

I'm not a perfect man and I never will be. I felt that if I released my stress, it would help me stay focused on my goals, aspirations and maintain my marriage, along with the secrets. My wife wouldn't understand that sleeping with other women and not being committed, stemmed from a diseased mentality. It was not her fault; even though, at times, I blamed her for my choices.

So I had to challenge myself to see why I cheated and where those desires to lie, cheat and hurt the one who loved me the most came from.

What had happened to me that I no longer cared about what I did, how I did it, and not care who had seen me do these things?
I had lost myself completely. I had to find what I never had; which is dignity and self-worth.

I had to terminate this illness within myself. I had to stop sleeping around to save my marriage. I had to save myself or I would never get a chance to truly love only one woman... I didn't wanna lose my wife!

Cheating was depriving me of God, real love and a well-balanced relationship. I had to find a barrier…a turning point because I was almost at a point of no return.

However, cheating became my way of life…and it consumed my every action as I watched the vows become meaningless and the marriage dissolve…And it was too late to say sorry.

THE CONFESSIONS BEGAN NOW......

I DON'T
WANNA LOSE
MY WIFE!
*(When it's **too late** to say I'm **sorry**.)*

BY **RAW**
(THE **CHEAT**OLOGIST)

"All I do is play and flirt
Chasin' every short skirt
Not carin' who I hurt
Or make feel like dirt...
Because she is just a woman to me,
No more than a friend...
Make love to her the first time and
Don't really care if I see her again."

CONFESSION 1:

MARRIED...BUT HAPPILY CHEATING

It was Saturday morning, about 8am, and the alarm clock did not go off as usual. But I woke up early anyway. It was the weekend, I was off, and I had planned to spend some quality time with the family. I looked over at my wife, who was still sleeping. "She is so pretty." I stated to myself while I sat up on the bed quietly, just staring and smiling at her. I have such a beautiful wife and I love her so much. I mumbled this silently, almost to the point of tears because something else was bothering me.

"Good morning daddy." My four year old son says as he climbs in the bed with us. My wife wakes up to my son's voice. She was always alert when she heard the children's voice. My two year old son shortly followed with "I'm hungry, mom." I love those mornings when both my children would jump in the bed, and my wife gets up to cook breakfast and we gather around to watch cartoons together.

What a good life! I loved the family feeling. The children knew with complete confidence that mommy and daddy loved them. But, on the other hand, they didn't know that daddy had some other issues going on.

Although all that sounded good, I compromised a lot. Not fully understanding the negative force behind my decisions to leave my family to be with another family. What made me choose other women, or chose to give something to a woman that was supposed to be for my wife only? We all tend to make apologies for mistakes, but an excuse for conscious behavior is unacceptable.

Most men, like myself, always wanted to be that perfect man; assuring our mate that we are not like the other men they may have had in their past that hurt them. We start off trying so hard to prove that we are going to love them better, but we end up hurting them more because we don't understand what love really is.

Some of us have no idea of how to love a woman beyond passionate love making. Even after the passion dies down, we claim a feeling that we can't confirm with our actions. We have no clue. The lack thereof in our relationships causes us to feel insecure as men, so we seek other women to make us feel manly and wanted at that given time.

We don't want to admit it, but we cheat our spouse out of a faithful marriage because we claim that we are being taken for granted. If she neglects to meet our demands, we look for a way to start an argument, something to justify our behavior. Now we exploit that situation and the cycle begins...This cycle repeats itself until there is no end in sight.

The relationship weakens, the trust is gone and the love becomes questionable. The man you once adored and loved becomes your worst enemy. He begins to stop caring about you, neglect home, disrespect you and lie. He regrets coming home, and prefers to be out in the club, on a secret rendezvous with his lover or just simply to avoid contact with you.

He becomes inconsiderate of your feelings, selfishly pursuing other women, and really begins to enjoy this double life. He is actually married, living a single life; but also happily cheating.

"This is my life, this is my confession...

To cheat one time is too many times,

But for me to make wrong choices

And to err was human...

But for my wife to forgive me,

That would be from God."

CONFESSION 2

PERFECT MARRIAGE.....NOT!

Let me admit something right off the bat; I am human and I am not perfect. We all make mistakes and bad choices sometimes. I just made more bad choices than she did in the marriage, and didn't want to fess up to my mistakes. But now, I'm admitting it: I sought affection outside my marriage!

I thought I was still a good man because I took care of my family. I provided for my home, spent time with my wife and children. I even worked hard enough to buy us a nice home, cars, and maintained a steady bank account. So how can you say I'm a bad man? If I stepped out a little bit on my wife, didn't I deserve a little freedom and play time, besides commitment all the time?

Married life bored me sometimes. The excitement of not knowing kept me pursuing things beyond my marriage. The excitement of other women screaming my name in ecstasy was fulfilling to me, and I loved it.. This excitement really became dangerous because I started to lose respect for my wife, my family and sadly myself.

I thought I was doing something worthy for my person but the lies, late night creeps and all the sexual advances upon other women were destroying the spirit of me even having a conscious. This left me blinded by my passion and enraged by my lust. There was no longer a truthful bone in my body left for the marriage.

Once I cheated on her, I could not stop. Something inside of me made me love this double life. At first I thought it wasn't that bad because I only slipped up and slept with one female. After that fling, I came to a conclusion of stopping my ways and I became more focused at home. I was sincere; well I thought I was sincere.

Shortly after I felt I had changed, I found the opportunity to cheat again. Something inside of me gave me the feeling that cheating was ok, as long as she didn't find out. I took comfort in being a good man in the eyes of my wife, but behind closed doors I was an unfaithful man wallowing in self-pity and guilt.

The more I involved myself with other women, the more I accepted the reality that I had a commitment issue. I would not be faithful in a relationship because I couldn't be faithful to myself. I couldn't be faithful to myself because I have allowed myself to be weakened by my desire to feed my flesh and starve my spirit.

Everything the other woman wanted was easy for me to accommodate because it took little effort to cheat. It was harder for me to stay faithful to my wife because it demanded my time, my energy, my attention, and my effort. Something I was no longer willing to give.

It became easy to deflect responsibility for my imperfections in the marriage because I assured myself that I was not perfect.

So how can I have a perfect marriage, when nothing was perfect.

"People don't cheat by chance, they cheat by choice."

CONFESSION 3

WHY DIDN'T SHE JUST LEAVE ME?

To justify my cheating ways I would always try to paint a bad picture of my marriage or of my wife, indirectly. That was the game I would play with words, in order to have the other woman to be a little sympathetic towards my request of her body. But I was deceiving my mistress as well. I would always speak negative about my wife so my mistress would feel pity and pacify my wants and desires.

A lot of women didn't even care; they just wanted a good fuck. I lied about the lie that I tried to cover up with a lie, to make it sound true. But they were all lies.` Sounds confusing, huh? Let me clarify....

I lied so that I could avoid the truth because the truth would hurt more than the lie itself. So I would lie and double coat the lie with more lies. I confused my wife with so many lies that I started believing them myself.

My wife had no sincere conviction of what I was doing with other women. Well, not until the other women started to return my wife's calls. My wife would call the numbers and whoever would pick up the other line, she would scream "Why are you sleeping with my husband? Are you trying to break up my family?"

What I couldn't understand was some women knew I was married. So why would they act as if I hurt them and flip out on me, as if I disappointed them by them discovering her call? Women play serious games too.

The women who really wanted to be in a monogamous relationship with me stopped dealing with me all together. They wouldn't answer my phone calls, they wouldn't open the door for me, and if I would see them passing by on the street, they would avoid eye contact.

I felt bad that I lied to some women. I was so into making amends with the women that I had lied to, but still not willing to focus on home by making that better and right with my wife.

Here I am with this "big head" and self inflated pride, like "I'm the man." But I was a damn fool! While boldly and impudently parading the other women around, I thought that was something to be proud of.

I didn't see it at first, but the women dealt with me on my terms because they were getting something out of the deal. On the other hand, all I was getting was a nut.

Women would sex me like crazy and it wasn't hard for me to get the woman of my choice. Not all of them were a dime piece, but they had something in common. Either the physical was bangin' or the head game was crazy. But again, none of that mattered because I was so into thinking I had it made, that I was getting played.

All the things the other women were doing for me, my wife actually did better. I only deceived myself into thinking that I was getting something better on the streets than at home.
A good meal, good conversation, and good sex; then, "Goodnight.... good morning... can I have this and

that? I need my hair and nails done. Can you help me pay my cable bill? Car note?" Always something!

Here I am chasing ass, lying and arguing in defense of my flagrant behavior but paying bills, tricking with other women and spending all my hard earned money on pleasing them, all for what? My lust was out of control.

My desperation has made me one of the dumbest players in this cheating game. I was on the path of destruction as my naughtiness pierced the heart of my morals.

I was not worth the good woman my wife was.....Why didn't my wife just leave me?

"YOU ARE STILL SO DISRESPECTFUL."

I really was feeling bad about what I was doing. Not just the cheating, but the apparent affects I was having on my wife's emotional being. Her crying episodes, her constant accusations, her nagging insecurities and her disgust with me; you could hear it in her voice, and you could see it on her face. But it was getting to me because she sensed what I was doing. Yet she allowed me to get away with it.

I took advantage of her fear. I knew she feared leaving me because I knew my wife suffered with the notion that she was worthless...like "Who would want her now with three kids; a daughter by one man and two sons by another?" She feared starting over; she feared stepping out on faith; she feared being called a failure by her father, and I knew this...And I played on this. One minute, I wanted to save our marriage; but on the other hand, I wanted to have the option to choose. Why did I think like this? What made me think that was right?

We went bowling, took the children to the museum, movies and to the park. But who would ever think I would be so low as to be out with my family and still feed my desire and urge to cheat.

I met Tanya when she was out with her sons at Chuck E. Cheese. All it took was a fatherly demeanor with my sons, like I was a family man, and a honorable-husband like attitude with my wife; that alone attracted Tanya to me.

My wife had the boys on one side of the game room, while I told her I had to go to the bathroom. Meanwhile, Tanya and I were exchanging numbers and glances that visually confirmed that getting up later, without the kids, would be in our plans.

When I got back to my family, my wife asked what took me so long. I made a quick excuse, but her facial expression showed me she didn't believe me. When Tanya walked by with her boys, I tried to turn my head and not stare but my wife caught me staring out my peripheral and shook her head, saying "You are still so disrespectful."

CONFESSION 4

**TRYING TO CHANGE A MAN
WHO DON'T WANNA CHANGE**

My marriage was no longer exciting to me. My actions began to denounce my vows. The energy of loving one woman became dormant and the idea of individualizing my fantasies of illicit passions became prevalent. My moments of seclusion were my escape from the responsibilities of the married life.

My wife depended on me too much, and that became annoying to me. When she knew I was upset about something, she would say how much she loved me, how much the family needed me and that she wouldn't know what to do without me. It was like she needed my approval for everything. Despite my infractions, my wife was still very loving though.

I would stay out late, sometimes all night. I would lie to her about almost everything and she still stayed with me. I took my wife for granted and the discourtesy was uncalled for. I can only now imagine her discontentment, and how I robbed her of her serenity.

So many lies, so many alibis and so much deception, yet she stayed with me as if nothing ever happened. For sure, we would argue and she'll throw things up in my face. But I would simply respond by saying *"I thought we were over that."*

How could she be over me lying to her and cheating on her? What made me think that just because I said I'm sorry or try to materialize my wife with gifts would make her pain go away. It didn't.

My wife covered up the anger and disappointment real good. My wife just accepted the flaws without challenging me anymore. I guess she got tired of crying, fussing, and trying to change a man that didn't want to change.

"I knew my wife depended on me to rescue her from despair; even though I was the one who caused it. I'd stay out til early hours of the morning; then I started coming in the next morning, then the next few days... creeping with different women and showing signs of a man that didn't want to be married."

CONFESSION 5

"I WAS A HOPELESS CASE"

I have to let you know that I did have a heart, and I did have a conscious. I did feel disgust when the scent of other women were on me; when I couldn't kiss my wife because of the other woman's orgasm that splashed my face, the odor left on my mustache and in my beard. Even though I washed my face good, soap…soap…and more soap, it still gave evidence to my wife that I was trying to cover something up. I did this so much that my skin was so soft and smooth, and washing my face became a ritual…to kill the scent of another woman.

There were times when I came home, after being out so late, and fucked my wife so good that she assumed those were signs of me trying to save our marriage. But that was not the case. More than likely, I had taken a stay-hard pill that preserved my hard-on till I got home. So I had no choice but to fuck till I softened up.

Oh yeah, I took them stay-hard pills even when I didn't have to. I had no problem getting hard, staying hard nor fucking for hours straight. Not bragging on myself, but I was a beast in the bedroom. Yet still, taking the pills at that time just became a habit.

I walked around hard all the time so other women can see my big bulge in my pants; I was sick. I wanted other women to want me, to desire me and to lust after me. Even having a wife at home didn't stop me from the "so-called" need to pursue other women, pop them pills like M&M's candy and eagerly fuck other women. I was sick. Not just metaphorically, but literally.

I'm sure the use of all those pills contributed to my chest pains and high blood pressure later on. Yet still,

I was so damn eager to fuck myself to death, literally that I kept popping them pills so I can endure long sessions.

I was seriously a sad case. I actually thought just because I was still sexing my wife, like crazy, that I was doing her a big favor. But I was doing her a disfavor, and I was doing her totally wrong. It was just plain immoral and I had no justification for my transgressions—none whatsoever!

But why did I continue? Well, the reason I continued is because my wife continued to put up with my nonsense. Even when I thought I covered up the tracks, my wife had to have a gut feeling that I was still out there cheating. She had to know, by now, that I was a hopeless case.

"I'm sleeping with different women, some have men and others don't...but I'm not using condoms with these women, and I'm kissing and licking on these women, openly and recklessly."

CONFESSION 6

A MONSTER IN THE MAKING

There are a lot of episodes that challenged the limits of my response to lust, as I deeply penetrate the threshold of passion. Here is one of them:

I can remember one freaky incident when there was a big icy snowfall in Richmond, Virginia. The next day the storm left icicles hanging everywhere. I had plans to meet up with one of my mistresses, just to take a stroll in Byrd Park to view the icy scenery hanging from tree branches. Crazy ideas started running through my head and I chased after one particular fantasy.

After meeting up with Michelle, we talked and walked in the park. We had an interesting conversation from politics to religion, to family and children. Michelle lived by Byrd Park in one of those big old houses that looked like a mini mansion. She lived alone too. Michelle was very professional, seemingly organized and very meek. I kept making her laugh and blush when I told her how beautiful she was.

I always had a way with words that made women open up more to me and feel comfortable, as if they knew me for a long time. I sensed when women were vulnerable too, and I often had them ready to play my game. I didn't tell them I was married if they didn't ask me. If I thought that question was coming up, I would change the subject.

Anyway, back to Michelle… we briefly talked about sex, but I cut the conversation short on purpose. Just to leave her a little curious about me.

Remember, I told you we had an icy snowfall that left icicles everywhere, and since she lived across the street from the park, we were able to gather various sizes of icicles and get them to her house before they melted. As soon as we got to her house, she put the icicles in the freezer.

We then stripped off our wet clothes and she kneeled before me like a servant, grabbed my shaft with her cold but soft hand and started sucking me enthusiastically. I knew this was going to be a night to die for.

After she relieved me, I told her to lie down on the floor and I went to the freezer to get a few icicles. When I returned, I found her with her legs spread wide open, wanton with lust. I snapped off the end of one of the smaller icicles and had her suck the end until it was rounded off nice and smooth.

Starting on the insides of her thighs, I rubbed the frozen dildo all over her; teasing her and then finally pushing it pass her pussy lips. The heat of her pussy sent up a little steam when it passed her pussy lips. She went wild, thrashing and rubbing her clit. After a couple of minutes of fucking her with the smaller icicles, I got a bigger one out. I had Michelle to round off the tip again smoothly.

As soon as I slid that icy monster in her she went crazy and had an orgasm. When she finished cumin' I slid my dick in. The feeling of her cold pussy was unlike what I ever felt before. I came almost immediately. We had sex that night until we were exhausted and totally satisfied.

I woke up at about 3am, took a shower and went home. I tiptoed into the room, kneeled down at the bottom of the bed and slid my head under the cover. I then licked in between my wife's toes and alongside her inner thighs until I got to her womb. I began to massage her clit with my tongue. She moaned, grabbed my head and raised her hips to fuck my face.

I would bring her to the edge of an orgasm and then stop. She would beg me to let her cum. I proceeded and she came like rain. We both rested and she never questioned me of my whereabouts and why I came in so late.

So after that night, coming in late, and she didn't beef, I entertained this twisted notion, in my mind, that it was okay to stay out late and fuck other women as long as I took care of home and kept my wife satisfied. Little did my wife know, she had created a monster.

SIGNS OF BETRAYAL

(A POEM)

I meet u here every weekend

Yearning to feel what I felt

Last weekend…

This is beyond physical, or is it?

I feel different when I'm with you;

It's like I belong here.

I have like a wild beast craving

For you…

For every inch of your body

Smelling every scent or it;

Licking every aspect of it,

Enjoying every conduct of it

And exposing every
shameful secret of it.

You belong to him, and I belong to her

But we belong to each other…..

Side by side, on top of...

My weight pressures your soft belly.
So I flip you over

And enter from behind...then flip you back over.

You scream in ecstasy

As I plunge you deeper...and deeper

We both erupt violently

And I collapse on top of you.

U dug deep in my back...leavin scratches.

My wife later saw these marks...

Signs of betrayal.

CONFESSION 7

WHEN BUSINESS BECAME PLEASURE!

I want to be as honest as possible with this confession: I don't leave my wife each day with the intentions to meet, greet and eat these women.

I have goals in life, and I make moves to aspire towards them. I meet different women every day, all day…I speak to flatter them because that's a method of sale: to make them feel open and comfortable with me. Next thing you know some questions take on a sense of personal inquiries; then business becomes pleasure.

Oh, I never told you what I do as a job: I sell clothes, shoes, boots, handbags… etc. You name it, I got it or can get it! Some people call me *"The Hustle-Man."* But after opening my first store, people seen my hustle became a business that people respected. So they looked at me as a **"business"** man.

The longer I sold clothes, the more persuasive I became. This persuasiveness became an art that leaked over into my personal life, and I used it to my advantage. Well, more like to my detriment.

I would go in and out of beauty salons with the intentions of selling clothes, but I would leave with money and phone numbers. Some women I'd call, others I didn't.

To be honest though, I may have dealt with three or four women that I met at a beauty salon. Other than that, I tried to keep my cheating real discreet because most women either had seen me with my sons, or with my wife, knew I was married and wouldn't even consider my gestures.

There was one particular incident, that I can remember so clearly, when I met Shawty. She was bad. Shawty always brought clothes from me, and she always had a way of flirting silently; like how she touched my hands, like how she would rub up against me, like how she bent over reaching for an item off my clothes rack; etc....

I just felt Shawty wanted me too. Shawty never asked to sleep with me for clothes, like some women indicated. But she did want me in that manner, I sensed it. With this in mind, we exchanged numbers.

This is when business became pleasure.

"As funny as this may sound, I needed to be with other women, outside my home, so that I may maintain a certain peace and need for me to be there."

CONFESSION 8

WHAT AM I DOING HERE?

THIS IS NOT MY WIFE....

I had plans to see Shawty about 9pm on a Friday night. We were talking with each other, off and on, confirming our plans to meet for a secret night of passion. I could hardly wait to see what Shawty had in store for me. She seemed too quiet to be a freak, so I was really unsure as to what this night would turn out to be.

As I was making my way over to her house, I called home to tell wifey not to wait up because my night was gonna be long. She said "Be safe out there, I love you."

My wife was so sweet to me. So why am I out here chasing other ass? Was I not content at home? That was on my mind, at first; then it quickly vanished as I replaced the thought with what I plan to do to Shawty tonight.

I stopped at Wal-Mart to pick up strawberries, whip cream and condoms. I called home to see if wifey needed anything from Wal-Mart. But instead of my wife saying *yes or no*, she began to question why I was at Wal-Mart when I was supposed to be on the grind. A brief argument aroused that ended in a dial tone.

"With her nagging ass." I thought. Wifey kept calling but I silenced the ringer…then after awhile, I cut my phone off completely.

I grabbed my throbbing manhood, I couldn't wait to see Shawty now. My anger at my wife made me want to fuck Shawty even more, with no shame and ruthlessly with passion. That's what made me enjoy cheating…the beast that I became in the bedroom, incited by the lust. I couldn't wait to get there.

Shawty called me a few times to see how close I was. I told her about the brief argument with my wife and noticed Shawty's silence. I figured that she did not want to hear about my wife and all she wanted was a good fuck. I am gradually learning how to enhance my method of cheating: less talk, more fucking.

Her voice was so calm and sweet but with a touch of idiosyncrasy…eager for the passion of the night. I assured her of my rush and whispered explicit things I wanted to do to her so she could get that pussy nice and ready for me.

Still on the phone with Shawty, I pulled up to her West End apartment complex and whispered "I'm here baby." I walked up the steps, the door was already opened, so I stepped in and before you knew it we were sucking each other's tonsils out.

Her tongue went in and out my mouth and I gladly accepted. She was so damn fine that I almost came on myself just looking at her. An hourglass figure, brown skinned, hazel eyes, approximately 4 feet 11 inches, 135 pounds, nice firm breast and had an ass as thick as peanut butter.

We continued to kiss passionately for at least ten minutes, non-stop. As we kissed, I began to run my hand up her thigh to feel how wet her pussy was. She was soaking wet. "Mmmmm" she moaned, as I stroked her clit. Her legs began to part more and more. She was squirming and making sexy little noises, telling me how good my fingers felt rubbing her pussy.

The more noises she made, the harder my dick got. It didn't take long for Shawty to cum, and she came hard. It was obvious that Shawty had that backed up sexual energy that needed to be released. She seemed stiff for a moment and then her entire body began to quiver as I was stroking her clit. With a long amazing moan, she pushed her pussy onto my hand and came, soaking my fingers with her juices. I sucked her juices off my fingers.

I let her recover for a few seconds, while I removed my clothes and her short baby doll ensemble. I sat on the couch and told her to kneel in front of me. She did so, meekly. I told her to grab my "fatt-man" and bang it on her tongue. She obliged my request.

As she banged my fatt-man on her tongue, while licking and slurping, I jokingly said to her, "You gonna let me cum in that pretty mouth?"

Shawty said, "Wait, I don't know about all that. I'm a lady; what will you think of me after this?"

Before she could complete her protest, she was licking and sucking my shaft, up and down, trying to fit all of me in her pretty little mouth.

Shawty licked, sucked and flicked her tongue back and forth on the underside of my "fatt-man."

She had almost taken me to my peak. She stopped, looked up at me with tears in her eyes and slid the rest of my "fatt-man" all the way down her throat. "Damn, that shit felt good." I exploded but was not done yet…and she swallowed it all.

I lifted Shawty into my arms as she pointed in the direction of the dark bedroom. I laid her down on the bed. She started teasing, "I don't wanna have you here too long, you know you gotta get home."

I ignored her and flipped her over, told her to get on her knees and then I felt her pussy from the back. She was even wetter than before. Her pussy was radiant with her juices. I turned her on her back spreading her legs apart, teasing her by running my tongue up and down her thighs to her wet pussy. I stopped short of her throbbing clit.

She moaned pitifully, "Please, please baby..." I abruptly slid two fingers into her pussy while I flicked my tongue vigorously back and forth over her clit. She came instantly. Her pussy contracted around my fingers and she called out my name..."Ohh, Raw. Ohh, baby!" She was twisting, wiggling and fighting me until, her whole body trembled as she drenched my hand and the bed with her cum.

This time around I gave her no time to rest. The taste of her re-energized me and I climbed on top of her and slid my "fatt-man" into that wet pussy hole. Amazingly, she was still cumming and her pussy muscles were contracting spasmodically. I lifted her legs over my shoulders, for deeper penetration, and fucked her hard and slow, plunging all the way into her and sliding almost all the way out.
Shawty was making sounds and noises that were unheard of, unable to speak complete words and sentences. She was so damn beautiful to me. Her beauty made me look down at her, smile and bury my dick

deeper in her bush. I silently heard her whisper, "Damn, baby! You can fuck this pussy all night." I felt a sensation go through me instantly when she said that. I knew I couldn't fuck her all night because no matter how good she felt, I had to go home.

Every time I softened up a little, Shawty had tricks that hardened me back. She was breathing very quickly and in a frenzy of anticipation. What was I in store for? Wait a minute! I thought...I have a serious freak on my hands. Shawty had took the jar of vaseline from the night table by her bed, and applied it on me slowly, up and down my fatt-man.

It felt really good the way she was stroking it, and massaging it on me. But when she then greased her fingers and slid them into her own ass, and began squirming and moaning in a fit of pleasure that became weird for me.

This was becoming very awkward because she kept asking me to put it in her ass, even after I told her I am not into anal sex. Shawty seemed a little agitated at my response. Then her phone rang, she put up her finger as to hush me, and she excused herself as she left the room. "Damn, you rude!" I replied.

When she returned to the room, she asked me to get dressed because her husband was on the way home. "What the fuck!" I was thinking, while she was throwing me my clothes.

I felt like I was getting played now. Here I am licking, sucking and fucking this woman as if she belonged to me.

But all along she had a husband. That passionate night turned out to be a rude awakening for me. I was married and slept with a married woman, who was probably sleeping with other men, unprotected. I felt like a fool again.

What am I doing here? This is not my wife.

"Men don't like to feel pressure all the time from their spouse,

So we sometimes cheat with a woman who doesn't sweat us like that.

I know that doesn't justify our behavior, but we start respecting our

mistress more because she appears to have a life, beyond us."

CONFESSION 9

MEN DO CRY...BUT IN THE DARK

Was I really feeling guilty because I was afraid that my wife would find out what I was doing and leave me? Or did I feel guilty because what I was doing was a great offense against the vows of matrimony? Was the marriage certificate just another piece of paper to me, or did the significance of spiritual values mean something? Could I really say that I love my wife, BUT still fuck other women, and claim unconditional love?

No! I couldn't. It was wrong. A wrong I could not erase out the pages of time. What I did to my wife follows me to this day. It probably would be the compass of all my relationships, but it shouldn't be. I hope it will not be.

There were times when I would come home, stand over my wife and just watch her sleep. Then I would walk over to the children's room and watch them sleep, and just kiss them on their forehead. I would walk around my house and just gaze at all the material success that I didn't acknowledge as blessings. I would so proudly boast under my breath, and in my heart.

But I had nothing. I wasn't anything but a filthy man with a warped heart and a perverted mind. And I felt this way. I would walk back into the bedroom, and watch my beautiful wife sleep and asked myself *"Why am I doing this to her?"*

Before you knew it, tears were forming in my eyes and I would cry...but only when the family was asleep...and only in the dark.

CONFESSION 10

ADDICTED TO CHEATING

I overlooked the symptoms and

my wife neglected to see the warning
signs.

I didn't want to accept the reality

of what I was doing.

So I would find an excuse…anything

to justify my actions each time.

I would use anger and obscene outbursts

as a defense to my weakness.

But I could no longer fight the truth…

no longer deny the illness

that was contaminating my mental.

I broke down…I cried for help.

The doctors could not prescribe a medicine

to aid my sickness……………..
I tried to stay in the house, away from the
Temptations…that suggested me to

succumb to my addiction.

I cold-turkey for days…weeks…months

shaking, shivering…a cold sweat at night.

My wife became my nurse at home

comforting and pampering me—"It's

gonna be alright, baby!"

But one day my wife left me

for an errand she had to run.

I thought to myself:

Maybe just one more "hit" for ole time sakes

But that last hit caused me my wife,

And my family—

and I was left alone

fighting an addiction

that is killin' me…

as my heart is poisoned by it.

Cheating was my addiction.

"I know that our women love us. But they are going to reach a point when they feel that they would do better without us, and decide to leave...Thus realizing that this cheating is a very complex issue for them to deal with because it opens up the door to greater problems. So we have to be men about this issue, and address it as men...the more we overlook it and don't get to the root cause of this behavior, it will have devastating effects on our children, family, and society as a whole."

CONFESSION 11

"Why I Lie And Why I Cheat..."

Why do I do it? That's the question that was driving my wife crazy. No matter what, she didn't want to understand why it was so important for me to keep certain truths from her. My wife also didn't know how the guilt was tearing at me, and how the constant lying was consuming more and more of my emotional energy.

I want to tell you why I lied about cheating, so you can understand my mind set. It's not really that complicated. I lied to my wife about cheating because it seemed easier than telling the truth. I lied because I was selfish and greedy, and I wanted other women without having to be accountable to my wife. I lied to avoid the unpleasant consequences of telling my wife the truth about something that I knew would have incurred her disapproval, her frustration, and especially her anger.

But why I cheated is often caused by something complex and more difficult to just jot down right now, and then say that's it! The reasons are buried deep in my unconscious and were shaped by prior life experiences, and what I have learned and believed about women, in general. Most of us men don't admit this because we are not eager to admit our faults and shortcomings. But there are many fears and conflicts in our own personal life that are outside of our awareness.

Just because I cheated, it didn't make me a "bad boy" or a "monster." However, when I chose to constantly deceive and betray my wife, my destructive behavior began and that's what made me a bad husband, and my disrespectful ways made me a monster. The more I confronted and questioned myself, the more truths about myself came to the forefront. The more closely I examined inadequacies, the more I uncovered the clues about what drives me to cheat.

It's obvious to me now, that all the lies I've unleashed on my wife came from a potent mixture of attitudes, perceptions, and needs intersecting with who I was, where I came from, and what was happening in my life at that time. Most of my lies were my way of warding off feelings and events that I considered threatening or painful. My lies served both to protect some of my needs and to shield me from a variety of unpleasant feelings, fears and consequences.

I couldn't explain this to my wife years ago, but now I see what I sort to protect by lying: my image that I wanted to project to the world, to my wife and to myself. I feared if I told her the truth she would have been left me.

I needed to be in control…I needed to feel I had the advantage. But it was sick the way my needs and fears were so interwoven, that my lying became a deeply ingrained part of my behavior. And that was because these needs and fears have come together in a way that made lying seem not only convenient for me, but almost mandatory.

My lies became abusive and intimidating, which led me to scream at my wife, cuss at my wife, grab and push my wife, and not even realize that I was totally violating her.

I came in late one night, and my wife had left a letter on my desk. The next few pages is a letter from my wife, crying out for me to stop hurting her.

51

"So here I am in the spin cycle...we're comin and we're goin
Nobody can know this...
And I was trapped in the house, lyin to my Mama
Thought it could get no worse as we maximize the drama
Started to call them people on him, I was battered
He hittin the window like it was me,
Until it shattered..... "

Song by Kelly Rowland
"Dirty Laundry"

Confession 12

A LETTER FROM MY WIFE
(in her own words)

Raw,

I hope this letter touch your heart, your soul, & your mind. I hope you understand were I'm coming from with this. I know people make mistakes, slip and fall, get up and brush the dirt off and try not to fall in the same traps that tripped them up. You seem to stumble with every step you take. In life we all have choices to either walk around the (lets call them) potholes, or keep falling into those holes. Satan jobs is to destroy a family. Think about it each hole in the road seems to be wider than the other ones you stepped out of. Let me make things a little more clear. Each woman that you come across is more pleasing to your eyes & other parts than the other. Satan knows what you want and what you think you need. He will give you what your heart desire. It's your choice to take what he is offering you. Every time you try to do good Satan widens the hole in the road and make his offer so tempting that you can't pass it up. You allow yourself to fall knowing that you have a family at home waiting for you. A wife who thinks you have failed me Raw. While you're in the streets taking care of your lust, passion and girls (I can't call them women, real women would not sleep with married men.) I don't want to hurt your feelings but you need to know the reason we are here. Those people that you do whatever with were sent to destroy you and me. Each time you allow yourself to be with another, you and them chip away our foundation. What we build I guess wasn't strong enough to withhold the blows that Satan was taking. Think about it you have cheated on me so many times, by having sex with others, by taking others out, by spending time and money on others. Those blows that I listed allowed Satan to step up and take over the marriage. While all of this was going on I could have left and never looked back. I could have taken the easy way out and left. I could have tried to get even by hurting you the same way you have hurt me. (but I didn't)

Before, I met you I had no heart. I would hurt people, and mistreat people just to get what I wanted. I destroyed a marriage, broken up a family and caused problems for people that I was supposed to care about. Then came you! After we got to know each other for the first time in my life my heart started to beat. When we got married I gave my heart to you and you made me complete. We had our share of problems Raw, ups and downs but we made it. Now our building, our marriage, our foundation is about to crumble. I don't know what to do to save this marriage. I feel that I'm working at it myself. It hurts because you don't see that. You always ask me what am I doing to save the marriage; Well, I was trying to hold on while you was doing you. Maybe I didn't go about it the right way by throwing situations up in your face, but you made sure you threw it up in minds(with the lies) was it all worth it.

How could you say I was a gift, when I felt like a curse. You say I'm your best friend. You betrayed my friendship and love by turning to others for comfort. All you had to do was love me the way you tell those others that you love them. I'm sorry I should not have said that.

Raw, I'm searching for those right words to say to you. I want to pierce your heart with my words so you can feel the hurt and shame that I feel.

Raw if you put love in your heart and your heart into love it will never fail you. We could have that marriage that we seek. (sorry, that I seek.)Love suppose to heal all wounds, but what am I supposed to do when my wounds are not healing and you are constantly throwing salt in them. Not caring if the wounds hurt or if they are healing I don't know what makes you do what you do but it has to stop not just for my sake but for yours. You are killing yourself Raw. Each time you commit an act outside the marriage God is taking away days off your life. You have children to live for. People come and go out of our lives for different reasons. I believe my purpose is to help you. How many women

58

do you know that would stick around?
There's a reason why I haven't left. God has a
plan for you. Please don't lost sight of your
future!

Those women know that you are
married and don't care. As long as you are
pleasing them and they are pleasing you
Satan's job is done. Our marriage...is it worth
saving? Can you truly be happy with me? Can
you only make love to me? Can you be honest
and open with me? Can you share your hopes
and dreams with only me? Can you promise
to raise your boys up with knowledge,
wisdom and understanding?

These are the questions that I'm sitting
here trying to answer. I know that you are
getting tired of reading and I'm getting tired
of writing. There is so much I have to say
but don't know how.....

<u>These are some things I promise not to do
anymore.</u>

- I will never, ever listen to your
  voicemail again. You have my word on
  that. It hurts too much to know that
  you keep on hurting my heart. You
  have broken my heart, but you haven't
  broken my spirit nor pierced my soul. I
  can be fixed. With the grace of God I
  will overcome all of this.

- I will not try to save the marriage by throwing your sons up in your face. If you cant be a honest man (husband) (lover) to me. Then don't prolong the situation. Don't feel bad about leaving. Some people fall out of love with each other over the years.
- I'm not going to look at the marriage and say Raw you did this to us. In order for a marriage to work it has to be something you believe in. I can say for myself I stopped believing when you stopped and stepped outside of it.
- I will not bash you in front of the children its not right, and I'm sorry.

I want to hate you, but my heart won't allow it.

See through all of the shattered pieces of my
heart it still holds a lot of love for you. No matter what we decide the love I have will never die. (LOVE NEVER DIES)
Search deep down inside of yourself Raw,
the answer that you are looking for is inside of your heart. It never fails.
Put love into your heart
And your heart into love...

(I will forever be your honi-bun and you will be my black knight who saved me!)

CONFESSION 13

WHY I LIKE TO FUCK OTHER WOMEN...

It's something about changing sex partners that did something to me. I had a hunger for passion that was unbelievable. No matter how good it was, I was never satisfied by one woman. It's like something I ran into ripped my moral tissue, and I didn't practice self-restraint. I tried to, but I just couldn't. So the matter at hand, why do I like to fuck other women?

Truthfully, I like the sense of power and control. I am always controlling the sexual encounters, either by stroking power or mastering positions. How the woman responds after she has those multiple orgasms; the way her entire body shivers, shakes and lose control like she's having a seizure. I love seeing that. I can't explain why, but there's something so sensual about it that made me a beast.

I really didn't have time to really love another woman and start a relationship. I had a wife, I had a family and I kept a busy life on the grind...yet still made time for affairs on the side.

Sometimes I would meet women at the club, where there was always potential pussy action; I would give them the eye and some responded with the nod. I never did a lot of chit chatting because either they was with it or not. I was never disrespectful either. I was always smooth with my approach.

Let me tell you again, I like me a good hit, quick and fast, you get yours and I get mine. We don't need to exchange numbers all the time because I really didn't care if I'd see them again. "That's why they called me RAW!" Raw attitude, Raw demeanor, Raw dawg! Get it?

Let's get back to why I like to fuck other women: I don't like the chase…I like the women who give it up easy. I like those who made me prove myself worthy too, but that was few. Sorry to say but a lot of women were too easy…too damn easy! One night stands were not only common but expected, at times.

I like to fuck, period. Who don't? I've dealt with all shapes and sizes. I like palming women's breast; I like making a trail with my tongue down to her belly button, pausing... just long enough to take a quick dip into it before I move down to explore between her thighs.

WAIT! If the pussy didn't smell right I would end that session, and she would never ever get a chance with me again. Never! But if the pussy smelled good as fresh fruit, before she could even prepare herself, I would take the clit into my mouth and begin to let it vibrate on the tip of my tongue.

The intensity of my licks made women cum instantly before I even ate the pussy, in which I knew women secretly hoped for. I didn't eat all the women I fucked, just some of them. Well, a lot of them but not all of them.

I never lacked sexual skills, and my wife didn't either. I just kept putting my sexual hunger for other women in front of other priorities; which was not the right thing, nor the mature thing to do. Just as much as I loved my wife, I loved the life I lived behind her back: fucking other women.

The truth is evident today I could not have loved my wife and then love to do the things that would help destroy her emotionally and psychologically. I was wrong, and she didn't deserve what I would soon put her through.

CONFESSION 14

I'M LOSING YOU...

I guess it's deception on my part

When I hide the true intentions of my heart

I tell other women that I'm single, when I

wanna hit it.....Then once I get it,
 I tell you "I wasn't with it!"

Passion yokes my conscious, then punch
morals in the face
My heart race...so I chase

Sin like a friend, then grab it real tight
Hold it like I love it, then I lose sight...

Of what really matters most

And to make matters worse...

I lie to cover up a lie

I really wanna stop the tears that
 overflow in your eyes

I intend to qualify our time
Yet on the grind, lust makes me blind
My foul heart then leads me to indecent
crimes

I now see me abusin' you...
The intimacy stops, so I'm refusin' you
Take you for granted, start using you
Now, I'm losing you.

CONFESSION 15

"I DIDN'T WANT HER TO FIND OUT LIKE THIS!"

This was a relationship that went beyond the call of lust. It was about pride and the pursuit in the name of "the game." Not saying I didn't get my feelings involved, but not as deep as she did. She was playing a game too, but it backfired on her. Her name is Vaughn. A thick cutie, caramel complexion, outspoken, church going, had kids, and a very conceited type of attitude.

A few times I solicited her attention, but only to get her nose up in the air as if she took joy in seeing me pursue her. I only thought about her when I would see her in the beauty salon. I never thought about wanting her, never fantasized about her or thought about sexing her, or even loving her. But once we got together our chemistry was so amazing.

Vaughn played hard to get. I didn't sex her on the first night, and I didn't feel that type of vibe from her. She was different. We would talk for hours on the phone; go to the movies, dinner, concerts and stage plays together. I was everywhere with her as if I didn't have a wife. No respect at all, for my wife, my mistress or myself.

I was a bad boy. I'm sure other people, who knew I was married, shook their heads in disbelief of how I was flaunting my mistress. I was seen at Red Lobster with Vaughn, by my brother-in-law and his wife. His wife made herself known and asked me in front of Vaughn, "Where's your wife? Where are the children?" I looked real stupid in the face.

I tried to play it off by ignoring her. But immediately after seeing them, I went into the bathroom and texted my wife. I told her I was picking up dinner from Red Lobster, so don't worry about cooking.

At first, that whole night Vaughn had a funny attitude towards me, but didn't once ask me about my wife. Arriving at Vaughn's house, we sat on her porch outside quietly. When I started to get up and leave her, then she cried about my deception and questioned me about my wife. I was now in defense mode.

I told her that I wasn't really married...that I just called my baby mama, my wifey. I told her I was having problems at home and that I wanted out of the relationship, but I had kids with her that I just couldn't leave. I made a lot of justifications and lies, rationalizing my situation, in order to hide the truth that I was married with children.

I knew I was really the problem and it wasn't my wife. I put my marriage on the back burner so I could please another woman who wasn't really into me. I pursued her because she played hard to get. It took months before I could even smell the fresh scent of her bottom. But once we started fucking, we met every weekend at the hotel. Friday night, Saturday night, and I came home to stay Sunday through Thursday.

This went on for months and months. I was out of control. My wife argued, cried and fussed. It was too late to dismiss Vaughn because I was in way too deep and I did what the fuck I wanted to do. I fucked who I wanted, when I wanted, and how I wanted.

When my wife questioned me, I exploded. That was my way of avoiding the questions and the truth. But when my mistress questioned me, I fucked her brains out until the questions ceased. They really stopped coming when I ate her pussy like there was no tomorrow. I noticed myself beginning to cater to my mistress and her family while ignoring the needs of my own home.

Doing the simple things like grocery shopping for her house but not my own home; paying bills at her house, but not my own home. It was becoming a responsibility to show love to my mistress, although I didn't actually love her. I was caught up in a fling that became a big and bad thing.

Vaughn moved into a nice townhouse. She kept me intrigued and that is what honestly kept me there. We never really argued and fussed; we always had fun and acted silly together. Me, her and her children, yeah I said it "her children."

My boys were just about three and five years old when this started happening. So I thought they were too young to understand and be affected by my unfaithfulness. So I continued to disrespect and argue my wife down about prying into my business. *"Ain't nobody cheating on you, stay out of my face with that…I'm on my grind, out here."* I would say to my wife. That was my argument and I was sticking to it.

She knew it was more to me staying out all night, every weekend, and I actually thought I was hiding it. Then it all surfaced one Sunday morning: I came home from the hotel and left the hotel card-key in my jeans. I was tired and got home about 8 a.m. My wife acted like she was dead asleep. I took off my clothes and crawled into bed....Moments later, snoring away. My wife jumped up, and started playing Columbo, looking for clues to my whereabouts.

My normal routine would consist of emptying my pockets and checking for anything that would give her a reason to accuse me of something, or suspect where I may have been. But I slipped up this time, and she caught it.

A few hours later, I woke up to her loud cry. *"You fucking cheater, liar, I hate you!"* I was trying to wipe the cold out of my eye, when all of a sudden I felt a slap across my face.

"Where were you last night," my wife sobbed. I'm still in amazement "huh?" I asked.
"You can't lie about this one, ohhhh I hate you. How could you do this to me?" she screamed frantically.
After getting myself together I said *"Yo, what the hell are you talking about?"*

She threw the hotel card at me and empty condom wrappers that she evidently removed from the hotel floor. *"I got this from your room, you bastard."* she yelled.
"What are you doing? That's not even mine." I screamed at her.
"I got a printout of your bill from the hotel." she said.

Damn! I thought silently, I was busted. How could I avoid this one? Not only did she go through my pockets and found the hotel card-key, she went through my cell phone and called all my last calls until she got to

Vaughn's number. How did she know what number to call and question about last night?
Talking about a woman's intuition...DAMN!

When I called Vaughn, she told me that she told my wife everything. And everything entailed everything about our affair.
Vaughn was like, "You could come here if you need to." Laughing like that shit was funny.

But Vaughn just didn't get it, this was it. It hit home. Now that my wife's convictions and beliefs were confirmed by another woman, who described me to a tee, there was nothing left but to leave Vaughn.

My wife told me that Vaughn described everything about my body, dick's thickness, length, down to the birthmark on tip of the head; that I like to hit from the back and that I mastered eating pussy. My wife was ecstatic, *"You are eating them women pussy? And you come home and kiss me and the kids? You are so fucking nasty."*

I was sitting at the end of the bed, looking dumb in the face. There was nothing I could say, nothing I could do. I tried to reach out and comfort my wife, but she pushed me away, slapped me again, and said *"You disgust me."* I was emotionally exhausted, but relieved in a way. Now she knows the truth... but I never wanted my wife to find out like this.

CONFESSION 16

A MESSAGE TO THE MISTRESS...
(and the other women)

I wanted to tell you this face to face, but time didn't permit. So I'm writing this brief note to you, hoping you understand where I am coming from and why I must come clean about this.

This may sound foolish, but thank you. Thank you for your kindness, your thoughtfulness, and your listening ear when I needed to talk about the problems I was dealing with at home. You made me feel good about myself and that's why being with you was fun. I have enjoyed our time together. That makes this more difficult to say and having what we are doing come to an end.

Our romantic endeavor crept up on me, and I wasn't fully prepared for all that this would entail. One moment, I can't wait to see you, touch you, kiss you, taste you, feel you... But then I feel wrong about pleasing you and neglecting my wife. I'm unsure about us, and my uncertainty should not be your problem. With that in mind, I think that it's best to put the brakes on this affair. We are running too many red lights and stop signs.

I couldn't put insurance on this affair because it was like driving a stolen car. I didn't belong to you and eventually we would have to pull over and make an exit. We have reached a dead end, and unfortunately this is where our road ends.

YOU CAN'T RIDE ME ANYMORE.

CONFESSION 17

GOOD SEX...DON'T EQUAL HONESTY

Now I was seriously involved with my mistress. Not just a quick lay, but feelings got involved. I never thought I would side with the other woman, but I did. My wife cried to make our marriage work, but I was tired of living this double life. I stopped sleeping around with different women, to be with my mistress and my wife. Then it became my mistress and not my wife.

My mistress tried to intentionally break up my home, with the hotel incident, so I had to end our relationship. My wife should be first anyway. However, I was stupid. Even after my wife knew everything about this affair, again she stayed with me. I promised her that it was over for good though. When I still crept around with my mistress, it wasn't the same. The excitement was gone. The passion was dead.

It all came clear to me that I had deceived myself into thinking that my affair was better than my marriage, when I was honestly benefiting nothing from cheating. I benefited nothing from creeping, and living this double life I led.

A full year took place and I stayed home to keep my family together, and my wife had my full undivided attention. Even after a year of living the family life, my thoughts of my past addiction left me feinin. I wanted to step out one more time. Now my wife and I had something in common. We were both lying to ourselves and each other.

My wife readily comforted herself with lies when the trust in our relationship began to vanish. She didn't want to face the fact that I was cheating again, so she resorted to the very same defense; lying, but to herself. She used denial to keep the truth from herself; she played a subtle but crucial role in perpetuating my deceptions. Now she's engineering the betrayal in the name of love, trust and saving the marriage by looking the other way and pretending everything is okay. So I was a liar, and she became the pretender.

My wife began the **"see, hear and speak no evil"** approach. When she seen a sign of me cheating, she turned her head away. When rumors surfaced, she turned deaf ears, and she never spoke about it. She avoided the facts that were deeply troubling her. I saw it on her face and didn't address it because I didn't want to start the drama all over again.

I also saw her silence as my ticket to keep riding the cheating trail. When my wife ignored the clear evidence and neglected the truth, it was like giving me a license that had been suspended. I am by no means blaming my wife. If it hadn't been for me making her feel this way, then she wouldn't think this way and feel insecure about the marriage.

I took her for granted once again. Even though I took care of home, I was still willing to have an intense sexual relationship with another woman. My sex life at home was wonderful, passionate and exciting, but that easily obscured the other facets of my marriage that I neglected. Like honesty, respect, sincerity, faithfulness and loyalty.

My wife began to equate my good love making with my love and devotion to her. But to the contrary, I felt no correlation between the two. Good sex didn't always equal honesty...And I definitely wasn't being honest.

"I tried to make the tremendous pain of

unfaithfulness seem like a paper cut...

I simply got tired of lying, so I confessed.

I wasn't actually taking responsibility for my actions;

Just evasive responses aimed at placating her by

minimizing my guilt."

CONFESSION 18

THE THRESHOLD OF GUILT

I wanna wipe my slate clean

I'm sorry for all the lies

About my lust that made me fein

I treat the other woman so nice

But treated wifey so mean

Treated her like my queen

But wifey like a freak

Was so committed to pleasing her

And never let wifey reach her peak

Would tell wifey to shut up

But so eager to hear her speak

Never wanted to be seen with wifey

But flaunted her around town

Stop surprising wifey with gifts

Because I was splurging money around
A store receipt for something I bought her

But not my wife...

Wifey found another clue of me living trife

I'm up to my neck with lies and deception

My license to lie was my confession

It's true, I took off the ring

To have a brief fling..

I promise I would never see her again

I stop seeing that girl only, but I had another friend

The threshold of my guilt overflows…

But will this cheating ever end?

"No matter how good of a woman you are, you will never be good enough to a man who isn't ready."

CONFESSION 19

I CAN'T BELIEVE I HIT HER

I don't want to ever justify my wrong doings but I will say, I am a product of my environment. The circumstances of my relations with different women would always dictate how I'd treat them.

What I mean by that is, either sex was the only thing we had in common or that woman could benefit me somehow. That depended on her emotional maturity, her sex appeal, her financial status and her good credit. Yeah, I said it. Ain't nothing like fucking a woman with some good credit.

Nah, I was just joking there. Good or poor credit didn't matter because I always held my own and rarely did any of my mistresses do anything to boost my financial status. I was a go-getter, and the women knew that; this is why getting women was never a problem for me. The problem was I couldn't stop, even after marriage.

I hurt my wife terribly; to the point she developed a tolerance for my lying and cheating. She didn't care about rumors anymore, she didn't care about what time I came in, and she didn't care about me changing underwear two or three times a day.

But why did she stop crying all of a sudden?... Was she ready to go with the flow entirely? Can I bring another woman home now? Can I just stop lying, and just do whatever now?

Hell no. The reason she turned away from the onslaught of my betrayal is because she created another world in her mind. She was fed up with my shit, and she wanted out of this marriage.

I didn't believe it at first, until I started seeing different men phone numbers laying around…. *"Bill? Ax? Joe? Doug? Melvin?"*
"Who fucking numbers are these?" I screamed.
"Baby calm down." They are just friends." She said calmly.
"You just met these dudes recently?" I asked. *"Nothing to worry about. I would not cheat on you."* She said sarcastically.
"Stop playing with me." I said meaningfully.

The truth of the matter is she displayed a different mentality towards me like "what's good for the goose is good for the gander." Which in turn implies, *If I could do it, then she can do it too."*

But I couldn't deal with this idea about my wife wanting to go out to the club now, then weekends out of town with her girlfriends…when she really didn't have girlfriends like that. She wanted me to start watching the kids on the weekend so she could hang out. She did a crazy turn around on me.

Sometimes our arguments got so heated she would literally say "Fuck me" to my face, swing on me and even walk out the house. I really wasn't used to this, so my emotions sent me flaring. One time, we even argued about having friends and seeing other people. I asked her was she fucking kidding me. But she thought it was a good idea.
I replied, *"My wife with male friends? That's not appropriate."*

Then she came back, *"Oh, but you can have female friends...and even fuck them on occasions? That's a double standard."*

I thought my wife was either heavily drinking now or using some type of drugs, asking me these crazy ass questions about having male friends outside our marriage. Like the great words of Big Daddy Kane, "What you on, huh, dope or dog food?"

But my wife was serious now, about me having female friends and she would have male friends....

"...And if I wanna fuck'em, you shouldn't have a problem with that because you've been saying 'Oh, she just a friend' and fucking them since we'd been married," my wife said confidently.

I was sitting on the couch in the living room, when she came over to me, bent down right in my face and asked sarcastically, *"It's okay to fuck friends as long as you don't find out, right? Ain't that's how you did it?"*

I jumped up, and my reflexes pushed her out of my way. She fell down and hit her head on the side of the wall, and immediately started crying. I stood over her, grabbed her by her neck and said *"Bitch, I wish you would play me like that."*

Before you knew it, we were fighting on the floor. She was screaming, scratching and kicking when I positioned my hands around her neck again, drew back and balled my fist to hit her when I looked back and my three year old had walked in; he was standing there just crying.

I jumped up immediately, and picked him up. I don't know if my son was standing there all along,

90

watching us fight, of if he just walked up, but I couldn't let him see this side of me. All my children knew was that mommy and daddy loved each other and loved them; so we must be play fighting.

That's how I tried to play it off when I reached to help my wife up. But she pushed my hand away. She told me to give her child to her and not to touch her ever again. *"It's over between us. And I mean it this time!" she exclaimed.*

I can't believe I called my wife a bitch, tried to choke her and almost hauled off and punched my wife. We were seriously going at it, and I can't believe I hit my wife.

After thought: "Trying To Defend My Wrong…"

What makes a man hit his woman? What makes a man attempt to physically harm the woman he claims to love? What makes him even think about it?

I can't believe that it even reached this level with us. All that guilt was coming out in a form of violence. I was weak minded to even think that it would result to a positive solution. How could it when I totally disrespected my wife, called her out her name and continued on with this behavior because I could no longer hide behind my lies and deception.

I was tired of all the nagging, and her telling me what I was supposed to do and not supposed to do as a married man. "I'm a grown ass man!" That was my favorite comment. But those were only words because I was acting worse than a little boy who didn't know what to do when his "little peter" got hard.

I would run around and chase ass, get caught in a lie by my wife, and fuss with her about finding out my business. I didn't know how to love my wife; I just claimed it. It's no way I could have loved her and then hurt her in the same breath. It's no way I could have loved her and intended to physically harm her. It's no way I could have loved her…I didn't love me.

Now the words of R. Kelly are my thoughts ♪ *If I could turn back the hands of time…*♪

Now is when I realized I tried to love her, but I failed. I couldn't deal with my failure with my wife, so I had affairs with other women to make me feel like I was successful at making a woman feel good about me, only so I could feel good about myself.

It sounds twisted, but I failed in my married life-yet I was a successful cheater. How crazy does that sound?

Arguing, cussing, fussing...

All in the name of a lie...

Trying to defend my wrong.

CONFESSION 20

HOW LONG ARE YOU GONNA PUT UP WITH THIS?

If you have read this far in the book, I strongly advise you to take all that you have read to heart. This is a serious matter because it's destroying our families, and the society as a whole is affected by our behavior. Our women are feeling hopeless, frustrated and very confused. Our women are left to be comforted by either another man or woman. Can we even blame them for leaving us?

We lie, cheat, mentally and physically abuse our wives and treat them like an object, not a person. We sometimes catch sexually transmitted diseases and pass it on to our wives. We have a diseased mind which causes us to lie all the time. Then we have the disease of the conscience which haves us to act out what we think.

I have noticed that after years of cheating, I have become extremely persuasive in shifting the blame for my transgressions. I became emboldened by my wife's easy acceptance of my previous lies, which I continued to lie, even when I didn't have to. My wife continued to be lulled by the sincerity of my explanations for my suspicious behavior, even when my lies were sounding more illogical.

I believe it was the sense of invincibility that led me to believe that I would never get caught. Even when my wife had strong evidence, I was skillful in convincing her that she didn't see what she saw, and she didn't hear what she heard. I would say things like "You are imagining things and exaggerating." Thus, convincing her that she is the one with the problem not me.

Through her actions, I could see her submitting herself to me, and through her own denial she convinced herself that she was over reacting and the one at fault. The self delusion allowed the lies to go on about me cheating, and our marriage to go on as is, without being corrected.

It's important to be aware that confessing can be very seductive. For many men who lie, confessing can often be just another tactic we use to divert your attention from the magnitude and consequences of our lies.

It's easy to confess and apologize, if we have the intentions to continue to lie. Once you forgive us, over and over, it's like a license to keep on doing what we want. So now you have the difficult choice of deciding how long you are gonna put up with this.

CONFESSION 21

I DON'T WANNA LOSE MY WIFE!

I didn't realize how this willingness to cheat was such a burden on my everyday life. It was like a cloud of doubt that overshadowed me when I approached some women. Maybe not doubt, but something about my swagger threw up red flags to women, to be careful. But I was such a respectful person, confident in tone and conversation that it didn't always warrant me as shooting game.

This was also a problem for me; I could count on one hand, how many women I pursued sexually and never scored…seriously. I slept with almost every woman that I ever approached. ***"Like that's really something to brag about."***

Most women I approached gave me a sign of them being interested. Some were materialistic, so that was right down my alley; while some were religiously grounded, which I eventually uprooted.

No matter if it took weeks, months, or years, if I wanted you, it would be a matter of time and circumstance to make that possible.

Always remember this, and you will be better off: Women choose who they wanna fuck, who they wanna love or who they wanna be bothered with. We have little choice in the process. They either have to be attracted to our looks, how we dress, our conversation or how we approach them to determine "I'm gonna give him some ass." With this aforementioned knowledge, I used it to my advantage.

But what happens when you feel you are tired of running the same game, tired of paying for pussy, with time and money, and tired of the same ole' drama that comes with the territory? I guess the best thing would be to settle down, right? Yeah ok. That's the logical thing.

Yet, after weeks, months and years of being in that committed relationship, we are faced with that same conflict that troubles us, and that's the same routine… So we are faced with the same challenges; that's sex beyond our bedroom, beyond our relationship, and sex beyond our marriage…with either someone of our past, someone we always wanted, or someone we never knew but wished we could.

This was my situation over and over again. No matter how faithful I wanted to be, I acted on my thoughts and proceeded with kissing the lips of lust; which in turn, my spirit was comforted in the hands of infidelity. That was not good. That is not natural, to want sex beyond your marriage….but we act as if it is.

We lie to ourselves when we say it is "normal" to want other women and act on it. It may be natural to desire the opposite sex, but the greed of our flesh wants more. So we have a woman at home and want more, we prey on vulnerable women and we cheat on our wives; Even when we possibly have the best thing going. So what is it that causes us to cheat? This is so widespread that it can't possibly be answered by one man...I can only tell you what caused me to cheat.

So we are back at the matter at hand, the cheating husband…me. So now that my wife knows that this cheating thing in me is uncontrollable, she must decide if she is going to stay or take the children and leave.

I wanted to save my family, but would I? Why does the desire to cheat seem uncontrollable, when it's really not…Am I willing to really give up cheating? Can I be monogamous? Will she leave me? Can I save my family?

.......I DON'T WANNA LOSE MY WIFE!

"When you give a man all of you,

Thinking you will get something better in return,

Then you are actually giving him control over your life.

After time passes, you realized you didn't

Get what you expected out of the relationship,

So you wind up disappointed

Leaving the relationship hurt,

Emotionally depleted

And empty handed."

CONFESSION 22

I'M NOT WORTH IT

I'm looking for the best words to describe this

We're both consenting adults, so we shouldn't have to
hide this
You said you feel the same way, so let's decide this…

Being open and honest with one another
Instead, we always arguing with each other

I know this is not what you expected
Being disrespected…and somewhat neglected
My overtime on the streets and in the clubs had affected
A marriage that "Love" had once protected

But now we try to hurt each
With harsh words and loud tones

I walk out and slam the door
Leaving you crying home alone

And I tell you "I ain't trying to hear that shit!"
But in truth, me losing you, I fear that shit
Here come the threats of a divorce, we're so near that shit
I rush back home to wipe your tears and shit

Cause I never meant to hurt you
I know that I'm a flirt but never intended to desert you

I never meant to betray you, then run away
My unfaithfulness took all the fun away

Please put that gun away… cause I'm not worth it!

"I had become so obsessed with pacifying my weakness that I had become selfish and greedy. I was proud of my moral indiscretions, and, sadly, wanted others to glorify me for my wrongdoings."

CONFESSION 23

"...A TONGUE THAT COULD WRECK A HOME."

I know she wondered about me; was I good in bed, did I have a big dick, or could I eat that pussy so good that she would cry. I knew she was curious. It was burning her up, but she just wouldn't give into her curiosity. I wanted to confirm her suspicions so bad. But I had to be patient with this one because she was not giving it up that easy. Plus she had a live in boyfriend. *But that never stopped me before.*

I just had a desire that day to fuck this girl so bad that I would have done anything; paid anything. I always seen her in the beauty salon, but never ever asked for her name…until that particular day. I would always see her and just stare; sometimes lick my lips and say to myself "Yummy." And that's the nickname I gave her.

"Yummy" was a stranger to me, personally; but I just wanted her. So the first day I received her name, I let her know I wanted her. She said *"Good; because I've always wanted your chocolate ass too."*

Her sexy voice alone made me protrude in my jeans. That very moment I knew she wanted to fuck me just as much as I wanted to fuck her. We made plans to see each other that night.

I was supposed to hook up with Yummy about 8 p.m., on a Friday night; we planned dinner and a movie. Things went according to plans, and after the movie we went back to Yummy's house. All night we talked, no touchy-touchy stuff, and we never even surfaced the conversation about sex. Although it was on my mind all night, I still avoided revealing that.

But amazingly, when we got to Yummy's house, she went upstairs to get comfortable, came down and lit candles all through the house. The lights went off after the sounds of R. Kelly and Changing Faces filled the room:

♫Do you mind if I stroke you up (I don't mind), ♫Do you mind if I stroke you down, (I don't mind)...all thru the night♫(I don't mind...)

We started fondling each other, kissing passionately. I knelt down and began to pry her knees open, exposing her cute pussy, in her see- thru negligee. I began to kiss her knee caps. Yummy asked me to stop. I asked her why, then she said she felt guilty about this whole thing. "Guilty about what?" I thought.

I never asked if she had a man, or if she was married because we both just desired to fuck each other, that's it; no ties. But little did I know she was getting married the following week. My bad...I thought.

But I had Yummy's thighs so creamy right now, she just continued on fulfilling the passion of the night...just one week before she would commit herself exclusively to one man. I guess my job was to show her how to become a freak for her husband, or atleast what to expect from her new spouse. That's how I justified it.

I started running my tongue up and down the inside of her thighs, spreading her legs wider with my hands. Her pussy was soaked by that time. I pushed her back on the couch, removed her negligee, and then lifted one of her legs up. I wasted no time getting my eat on as the appetizer.

My warm, thick tongue flickered back n forth, up n down her pussy walls, and I know she got lost in the music that was playing:

♪ *Let me lick u up-n-down, till u say stop-let me play with your body, baby, till u get hot♪...♫ I wanna get freaky with you* ♫

I ate her goods for one hour straight, and she kept leaking like crazy....pouring like a water fountain. I didn't know if she could even take anymore; she came over 3 times....and was still ready to go. Damn, girl!

Yummy grabbed my dick to suck it, but I told her she didn't have to. I told her that eating that pussy was my gift to her. Then she begged me...literally, begged me to fuck her. But I didn't. I left her house with her yearning for me to enter her from the back. I left her in lust.

Couple years then passed now since that incident, and I heard that she is happily married with a child. When we see each other, we just wave, smile and keep it moving. I never discussed our secret until now. I regret having this secret...and this tongue that could wreck a home; that is, if her husband ever found out about our secret.
Sssshhhh......

CONFESSION 24

THE SERIAL CHEATER STRIKES AGAIN...

I was coming out of Fairfield Commons Mall, when I met De'osha. It was a hot summer day in July. She had a pretty bronze like complexion, about 5'8, a thick cutie with measurements that my eyes like. I don't know the science of numeric measurements but I do know a phat ass, big tits, a gap and a walk like she needed a good fuck.

So here I go: "Excuse me, miss. What's your name? Can I come? Can I take you home, tonight?" I was singing a hook from Jay-Z, but at first her facial expression showed a sign of disapproval. Well, until she realized it was from Jay-Z, then she smiled. I asked why the sad look on such a pretty face, and she replied she just got off work and was a little tired. "Too tired for dinner and a movie later?" I inquired. Her face seemed to light up a little, and she said "Sure, what time?"

"Let's say, I'll pick you up about eight o-clock, and we'll go to Virginia Center Commons...We'll get our tickets and grab something to eat." Then she asked "If it's okay, could we meet at the cinema?"

I told her, I was cool with that. It gave me time to finish up on my grind, go home and get my story straight. I knew already, from how her frown and weariness turned to a smile, that De'osha haven't been dating for a while, and the meeting was right on time.

De'osha was a cutie, but she was a little bougie with her dress code, how she walked and how she talked. But that was all good. I just wanted to go out on town with something new.

Remember, I was patching up things at home and working on my marriage. Wow! And I'm about to go home and tell my wife that I'll be in late tonight, again? No lies, no excuses…"I'm just gonna be in late."

I went home unusually early on Friday; mainly because I knew I had plans for later. I wanted to spend some quality time at home, to kill any suspicions. My wife cooked dinner and I didn't refuse a plate; I just ate a smaller portion of food. Now my wife always looked for signs to indicate my cheating, but I'm always two steps ahead of her questions and implications.

In the past, I wouldn't come home to eat when the hot food came right off the stove. Instead, I would microwave my dishes left for me when I came in late. I would sometimes eat a little, and throw the rest away. I was either full from dining out or either pussy juices mixing my taste buds that prohibited the natural taste of my wife's good cooking.

For whatever reason, she would look in the garbage can and later question me, in a sense of accusing me; that I probably dined out with one of my lady friends. I avoided that argument many times.

Well, after dinner my wife and I sat down to talk, and here we go again.
"What's wrong, Raw? "She asked.
"What you mean, I'm good." I responded.
"Then what are you up to tonight?" she said with a sadness in her voice.
"I answered your phone, while you were in the bathroom, and some girl named De'Osha said she is gonna be about 30 minutes late."

"Oh, ok. That'll give me more time to get her package ready." I said.

"What package?" my wife asked confusingly. "Oh, she wanted me to download some wedding songs on about 2 cds for a marriage reception tomorrow. And I'm gonna meet her about 8 p.m. when she get off work...."

"You wanna ride with me?" I asked my wife, hoping she said no.

But she said "Ok baby, I'll get the boys." Damn! I put my foot in my mouth though. How am I gonna get out this one? I was hoping she would say no.

My wife was excited to go everywhere with me, even if it was to the gas pump. Now that I was in the house more, she felt a sense of relief that I wasn't on the street chasing ass. But the truth is that I really wasn't chasing women, they were everywhere.

I would meet over three women a day, literally. So add up three women a day times seven, then multiply that times 4 weeks a month. This is the equation of prospects: *3x7=21 women a week, 21x4=84 women a month. Now out of 84 women, how many I slept with is the question.* The answer is disturbingly amazing.

So here I am now asking my wife to accompany me places, so that I could combat this urge to get other women's number. Cause more than likely, if I get a number, sleeping with her wouldn't be too far off.

This is what I mean by "creating the circumstance." Conversation is a ticket to flatter, and flattery is a tool to entice; to entice is to encourage, and to encourage is to suggest; to suggest is to request, and when you request you are asking for ... It's up to her to say yes or no, now or later, and when and where. These are the steps of "creating the circumstances to cheat."

Wifey came downstairs, and I asked what's wrong. She told me to go ahead because the children had laid down to rest after dinner, and she didn't feel like waking them up and getting them ready. I assured her I wouldn't be out beyond midnight.

"I'm just gonna make a few runs, then I'll be back so we could lay back, relax, watch a movie and make love into the morning."
She laughed and said jokingly, "Hurry back so I could put this pussy on you."

I then pushed her back on the couch, turned her around so her ass was facing me, bent her over the couch, moved her thong to the side and gave her a quickie. We both came quick... My wife said she was so fucking wet, so hurry back.

I stopped at Wal-mart, before I drove out to Virginia Center Commons. I got there about 8:45 p.m. I called De'osha about three times but she didn't answer. Just when I was about to pull off, she called.

"Sorry about that; I couldn't find a babysitter for my daughter. So I had to bring her."

117

"That is quite fine. Where are you?" I asked. *"We are pulling in."* She said more excitingly.

When she pulled up to the theatre, she parked beside me. I walked up to the car and handed De'osha flowers, and her daughter the teddy bear. They both smiled gleefully.

"And how are you?" I kissed De'osha's hand, and I shook her daughter's.

"The movies are playing rather late tonight, so how about we just have dinner and get better acquainted." I asked politely.
De'osha said "Good idea."

We had dinner, a good conversation and we promised to stay in touch. I called De'osha to make sure she got home safe. Insecurity again lurked in my home, until my wife seen me come through the door. My wife got up from the couch, went in the kitchen and fixed brownies and some ice cream; we watched a scary movie, and nodded off to sleep together.

About 2 a.m., I jumped up and made love to my wife till about 3:30 a.m. She told me how much she loved me. She actually cried and said *"You don't know how much I love you."*
The truth is, I did know how much she loved me. But I couldn't stop this desire to want to lay my head on a new pillow; this desire to hear someone else tell me how good my sex was. That was my get high; thinking about De'osha, who would soon be my next victim.....And the serial cheater is about to strike again.

"Our wives deserve our respect.

Our wives deserve our patience.

Our wives deserve us to be faithful.

Our wives deserve our attention.

Yet instead, we give these energies

into our affair,

and neglect home...

and our wives don't get nothing they deserve."

CONFESSION 25

WHY DID I EVEN GET MARRIED?

I started talking to De'osha at least three or four times daily, was meeting her out more, and just had a good time being with her. I kind of like "beat around the bush" about being married, at first. But then it surfaced in a conversation. Yet she didn't respond in the negative. She told me that she was married too but her husband was a nonfactor now because he was locked up. We never discussed him again.

So here we go again, another affair in the making…another one I could have prevented, but my ego got the best of me.

It's been weeks now and I haven't yet hinted at sexing her. I was taking my time, plus my wife really stayed on my mind. De'osha had such a sexy attitude with her, that I knew it wouldn't be long before we penetrated the silence of the nights we shared together.

I believe the reason it took longer than usual was because I was truly trying to stay loyal to my wife; and I kept this "Family First" demeanor, even in the eve of my passion.

I remember the first time when De'osha and I were ready to break the ice…we had seen a movie, and after that we went straight to the hotel. We went to the Comfort Inn off West Broad St. We had a nice suite, with a living room, jacuzzi, king size bed etc. a nice atmosphere to pipe my guest.

We immediately started kissing and fondling each other, to the point of panting like desperate teens ready to fuck in rage. But I calmed the passion and suggested relaxing in the Jacuzzi, while I played a seductive and suggestive song on the cd...

♪ *You must be used to me spending, all that sweet wining and dining....but I'm fuckin you* ♪*tonight.....Here's another...and another one.* ♪

So De'osha got the picture, and she felt my manhood enlarge in her hands as she stroked the huge bulge in my boxers. "Hmm is all this for me?" she said as she stroked ever so gently. I sounded like a kid in response, "Sure thing."

But even though my hard on made it appear like I was ready for this sexual match, my mind wasn't all there. I kept looking at my watch, thinking about hitting De'osha quick and going home to my wife. I kept saying to myself, *"I can't do this. I promised myself no more of this."*

But the more I thought about how good De'osha looked and how she was so hot and ready...but on the other hand my wife at home...Damn! How am I gonna get outta this?

After about 30 minutes passed, De'osha finished soaking in the jacuzzi, then went to rinse off in the shower. I was nervously laying in bed like this was my first time cheating. I knew it wasn't, but it just didn't feel the same. This time I really didn't want to cheat on my wife. So I was looking for an excuse to not do this.

Maybe I'll tell De'osha that my kids are sick and I gotta rush to the emergency room; or maybe I'll fall asleep; maybe just get dressed and leave while she in the shower; or maybe I'll just orally get her off and don't hit it…will that still be cheating? So much was running through my head, but then it came to me.

I told De'osha that I didn't have any condoms on me, so I need to go next door to pick up a twelve pack for tonight. But when she got out the shower, I almost lost my mind……
"Damn baby, I'll be right back."

Although De'osha body was model-like amazing, I still wanted to call this evening off because I really had conflicting emotions. I wanted to fuck so badly, but not De'osha…I wanted my wife. So I had to break the news to De'osha.

When I came back to the room, De'osha was lying on the bed, on her stomach, and her ass sitting up a little where I could see her slit enough to slide in from the back. And that was truly a passing thought. But I had convinced myself to come back to the room and tell De'osha that I wasn't feeling this tonight. I walked in the room and sat at the end of the bed, and rubbed De'osha's leg. She must have nodded off, because she said she didn't hear me come in.

"What's wrong, baby?" She asked.
"De'osha, you are truly a sight to behold, and I adore your presence in my life. But I just can't bring myself to having another affair on my wife. So please, get dressed."
De'osha looked at me, and said *"Why would you do all this, come this far and then shut me down like this?"*
"It's not you, it's me. I can't do this." I said to her.

De'osha was obviously mad when she told me to go ahead, and that she was gonna just lay there herself and relax.

I left the room, down the elevator and through the hotel lobby with tears in my eyes. It felt like I did something wrong, but I didn't. And it really felt good turning away from this situation. I was going home to my wife, where I belong.

Before I got home, I spoke with De'osha; she was upset and crying, saying that it was fucked up how I played her. She told me I was confused, and not to call her anymore.
"Very well, I said, you're doing me a favor." "And what do you mean by that? De'osha said in a snobbish tone. *"This cheating shit is getting to me, and I'm battling with it...you wouldn't understand."* I said.

De'osha told me I was a confused. I said *"What the fuck, I'm not confused...ain't you married too? Then you should understand."*

Then she said that the reason I keep cheating because it's my dissatisfaction with my own life that's reflecting off of bigger issues, that will never be resolved if I am not willing to accept that either I really don't love my wife, or I don't really want to be married.

It really made sense, even though I didn't want to hear that coming from a woman who was cheating herself. But was I fooling myself? I started to reflect on what she said. And I was left doubting and questioning myself, *"Why did I even get married?"*

CONFESSION 26

I CAN'T PROMISE YOU THAT I WON'T CHEAT AGAIN...

Now things were getting a little more complicated because my wife announced she was pregnant. I told her stop joking with me. But after taking a pregnancy test, almost every other day, claiming she swore the line was pink on the positive side of the test, this time it was actual fact----My wife was pregnant again!

I thought for sure she wanted to abort that reality, but my wife was happy. Me on the other hand, I was like "Damn. I don't want another child right now."

I don't know if it was because I knew I wasn't financially fit to take on another child, or another child would interfere with my double life. I mean, I loved my wife but what if I wanted to creep again. How could I do it to my wife and family again? It wouldn't be right.

My wife was so gleeful and on cloud nine; as if she won a championship bout. I guess she felt by getting pregnant, it was the punch that would knock the other women out the ring. However, that was not the case.

I pretended to be happy, at one point, but on another I noticed myself getting more impatient with her. I would mix up my wife's emotions by saying *"Have an abortion."* Then after her crying profusely, I would say, *"Nah. Keep the baby."* But back and forth, *"Keep it-abort-keep it-abort!"* It was a confusingly painful time for her; it was like I had her on strings like a puppet. I was totally in control of her emotions.

My wife wanted to feel a sense of victory: she was pregnant, and no other woman could have me now. I guess she needed some kind of assurance, that despite all that I have already put her through, she really mattered more. Maybe the new baby would bring us closer…Maybe I would stay home more.

I could see she was depending on me again, hoping that I won't hurt her. But I couldn't promise her that.

"A cheater's life is consumed by so many lies that he start believing the lies himself."

CONFESSION 27

BOTH OF THEM, PREGNANT?

"AT THE SAME DAMN TIME!!!"

I really started to feel bad about what I kept doing to my wife. It was becoming a routine: the way I would meet women, speak in a charming and humorous manner to flatter women, exchange numbers and persist on with the scheme to seduce their heart. Then once I got them open...I would *spray their walls* white. My lust had no point but to conquer its prey.

Sleeping around with different women became a ritual to the point of disgrace, which made my wife a woman scorned. I ignored her grievance which, in turn, depressed her more. I tried so hard to keep my lies a secret from her. I didn't want to hurt her ever again, but I seen myself slipping. She sensed I was cheating again. I continued to harbor thoughts in my mind about other women that would lead me to do things that would destroy her completely if my wife found out. Like, get another woman pregnant...

Yeah! I was married but got another woman pregnant. I had totally messed up the game now. I knew I was never supposed to get 'em pregnant...but that's what happens when you don't strap up. I completely went too far now. How was I going to explain this one to my wife, when I don't believe in abortion?

I was so damn stupid. I didn't always use condoms because I really didn't like using them. I like it raw, and those women loved it Raw! My excuse was condoms didn't fit comfortably around my penis. So, I guess I was out there itching for a damn disease. Do other men do this or am I the only idiot? Playing with my very own health, life, and my wife's life...over a nut?

My wife had every right to leave now because my wife was pregnant and De'osha was too. But even though my heart was heavily against abortions, I had to decide which woman to chose... who I could see a future with. I know, I shouldn't have had to chose, just like I shouldn't have been in this predicament, but I was.

The whole situation was confusing to me. After leaving De'osha in that hotel, and she didn't call me in weeks, I probably slept with over five different women in that short time frame. This is how serious my sickness was...I just wanted different women...I just had to have it!

Everywhere I went women was throwing themselves at me, giving that thang away like it was going out of style. Surprisingly, without ties and that was perfect for me, being that I was already married.
    Now here I am trying to work on my marriage, but I hooked back up with De'osha about a month later, had an affair with her for about eight months. Then before we stopped seeing each other she dropped the bomb on me, that she was three months pregnant and she is keeping the baby.

Even though I told her I didn't want a child, she said she was keeping the baby with or without me. I felt empty and shallow. I couldn't breathe. The more I argued and fussed about how the new baby would mess up my married life, that didn't convince De'osha to have an abortion. It actually magnified the problem.

Deo'sha was more eager to know, that by her being pregnant and my mistress, she thought I was going to leave my wife for her. But I couldn't do it. I shouldn't leave my wife for another woman. But sadly, I did.

Both of them pregnant, though? At the same damn time!

"Don't ever commit to a secret relationship because you may end up being the secret in the relationship."

CONFESSION 28

WHEN THE SHOE IS ON THE OTHER FOOT

At this level in my dealings, I have gotten worse off. I kept promising my wife one thing, but doing the other. She was getting tired of trying to hide a pain that was evident, and I was getting tired of lying. When dealing with the other woman, I acted as if I wasn't married, so my wife stopped pretending she was married.

I told my wife to get an abortion because it was no guarantee that our marriage would last. She was devastated when I told her that I didn't want to be married anymore. Then I would apologize and say "I'm sorry, I wanna be married but you pressure me too much. And you never trust nobody."

But how could she trust a liar? A cheater? An abusive husband? I had some nerves trying to act as if I deserved her respects, when I violated her status and her rights as my wife. My insolent actions sabotaged her self esteem. I slept around with women she didn't know, women that seen her, smiled at her and waved but was sleeping with me all along.

I honored my affairs more than my marriage, and I deserved it when my wife told me she didn't wanna be married anymore either. Even becoming a threat to her own life, she said she didn't even wanna live anymore because of me.

My wife said it hit her when she took a whole body of sleeping pills, fell unconscious in the bathroom, hit her head and was rushed to the emergency room. I think, her brother came to visit at that time and rushed her there. At least, that's what she told me. Come to find out, she was lying and just seeking attention. My wife started cutting herself and doing a lot of crazy shit; all in the name of "attention." Her self-esteem was at an all time low. So she started doing things to repair her self-esteem, and not caring what I thought.

Like for instance, she started creeping with her girlfriend's man. When I questioned her, she straight up lied. But her actions started to prove something different. My wife was transforming right in front of my eyes, and there was nothing I could do about it.

She began staying out late, not answering her cell phone, and wanting to hang out on the weekends and leaving me with the kids. Our sex life was dead. Our marriage was over, and our family was no longer a unit.

My wife began to disrespect me out rightly, and I couldn't deal with it. I even seen this dude drive her around in the car that I bought her. Hell no! This can't be happening. Now the shoe is on the other foot, and I couldn't take it!

"My wife no longer felt wanted or loved by me; she begged for my attention, and pleaded for me to start taking her out because she was feeling lonely...but I kept ignoring her. I left her vulnerable...and susceptible to the next man's influence."

CONFESSION 29

WHEN A WOWAN'S FED UP....
PACK UP!

I had a serious problem that became a habit, and that habit became a behavior that became a constant battle. My wife is suffering terribly though; she had fallen apart since she had the abortion. I felt so wrong to do this to her, but I knew at this point I could never be faithful to her. I was never faithful, and I didn't know how to be.

I wasn't capable of loving her because I didn't know how to actually love and respect myself. My guilt, my tears and my misery were just as superficial and contrived as all the other acts I put on before, and my wife seen right through me.

For weeks we stopped touching, kissing and having conversations. We slept in different rooms; we started living like roommates, and eventually, she asked for a divorce. She even had the nerves to ask me when I would be moving out the house. What? Move out the house that I bought? I wasn't man enough to just give up everything and start over. I really wanted to change, but it was too late. My wife had her own agenda now.

I ended the affair with De'osha. Due to the stress of our relationship, she had a serious miscarriage. She ended up hating me because the miscarriage made it impossible for De'osha to bear any more children. I hated myself for that.

I was really messing up people's lives, and mine too. But before the divorce was final, my wife did something to me that would change the course of my life, forever.

I was going to end this chapter with words from R. Kelly's song, "When a woman's fed up, ain't nothing you can do about it." But the truth is, when a woman is fed up, it's time to pack up!

CONFESSION 30

WHEN A WRONG FEELS SO RIGHT...

I tried to explain in Chapter 13, why I like to fuck other women? But as I write these confessions, more and more reasons come to surface.

I like the way women express their sensuality in the way they talk, the way they walk and the way they dress sometimes. I like women who are comfortable with their bodies because what counts for a man like myself is the body; to see it, to touch it, to smell it. I am a voyeur; I love to watch in lust.

I appreciate a mistress that is patient, never making me feel rushed during sex, and one who caters to my preferences, leaving me satisfied. She buys nice lingerie and strips it off slowly for me, like a stripper...And the mistress knows that's what I like. She dances for me, act out roles for me, and then climb on top and ride me until she can't take no more. "I loved that shit!"

Now in the beginning, my wife was the same; she made me feel warmed, loved and safe. She had always dressed sexy, was spontaneous and freaky; She also cooked and fed me good. Our sex life was mesmerizing. But when sex was no longer a priority for my wife, and she became more interested in being a mom than being my woman, it began to kill the atmosphere of love.

She didn't see it though, but when my wife pushed sexual love aside, when she stopped complimenting me and saying nice things to me: Like, how good I looked in an outfit, how good I smelled, how good the sex was and other simple things to put me at ease, I began to look for this from other women. My own insecurities set in.

A mistress loves to give a man what he feels he is missing at home. And when I felt I was being satisfied more outside of my home, that's when cheating became enjoyable for me. That's when cheating became compulsory for me; and that's when I begin to love to lie, to guard my double life. But once it hit home, my actions were no longer discretionary.

Are you still wondering why I kept cheating on my wife? Well, please understand that people change, and so does the need to maintain love. Why couldn't she stay sexy for me? Why couldn't she flirt with me sometimes? Why did I have to make an appointment to sleep with my wife?

Why did our good conversations stop? Why did she keep saying "All I talked about was sex?" Did she not understand…. "Hello! You are my wife….who else should I be talking to about my needs being met?"

I am not fully the blame for everything; she has to own up to some responsibility. But even if she did own up to the responsibility of depriving me, of some of the intimacy of our relationship, would that have prevented me from fucking other women?

Probably not because it's so hard to stop a wrong, when it feels so right.

"Be strong enough to let go of what is not good for you and patient enough to wait for what you deserve."

CONFESSION 31

"IF ONLY I KNEW WHAT I KNOW NOW."

How did my life get this confusing? I had a beautiful wife and two handsome little boys, born in wedlock; my wife looked good, cooked good, was a real good nurturer for the children, and I was content with our sex life; at first . What made me dissatisfied with what I was obviously blessed with?

I promised her father and mother that I wasn't going to hurt their daughter, and that I would love her until I couldn't breathe no more. But sadly, I am still breathing... but our marriage is no more... my love for a woman I'd been married to for seven years is done. How does this happen? How is it possible that the love for the mother of your children stops, just like that, when you both did everything together?

How will my children feel when they get older, read this book and witness the pain I caused their mother? Will they look at their father with love or disdain? I can't answer that, but the truth must be told and the secrets confessed with a purpose.

If you've read this book thus far, you should have learned to detect the sickness of infidelity early, and try to avoid the pain you will face and learn from my mistakes.

Even if you are not cheating now, once you cross that line of disloyalty, that line becomes very thin and we are prone to repeat habits...then habits form personalities. Personalities display different forms of behavior, often conflicting to its natural self.

I am not a psychologist nor am I a doctor. I do not have a degree on love and relationships. I am just a simple, everyday person like you...who had a wife and family, and cheated them out of a good life because of my selfish behavior and greed. I am ashamed to even mention all that I've done, but I had to write these confessions because I am no better than you...I'm just a man who finally had the heart to confess.

I wanted to stop cheating. I wanted to save my marriage. I just wasn't willing to stop what I was doing that helped to destroy the marriage.

I wanted to turn away and turn down solicited passion. I wanted to be emotionally mature and man enough to have one woman and pour my love into the cup of her existence, until it overflowed. I wanted the best for myself, just like any man should want for himself. But even with this knowledge and awareness, we find ourselves being challenged and sometimes weakened by the same circumstances we create.

So if we want to stop cheating, we have to change how we think and what we think about the relationships we are in, and about the one we claim to love. We must redefine in our hearts what we think love is, and redirect our habits of love.

Our women should not have to hurt or suffer because we as men fail to love them adequately. We need to mature, stop chasing and pursuing other women. We need to give our women the option to choose, if they want to stay with us after the painful discovery of our betrayal, instead of us perpetuating the lies. We need to stop justifying our behavior and man up to our short comings.

151

When we unite with our mates, build a family and nurture the children with the love of both parents, what do you think a divorce will do to the children? Do we even think about that?

If only I knew what I know now....

"If you cheat on a woman who is loyal to you and willing to do anything for you, you've actually cheated yourself out of true loyalty."

CONFESSION 32

HER METHOD OF REVENGE:

"HE'S THREATENING TO SHOOT ME!"

I can remember this as if it just happened yesterday. My wife left out Friday evening about 5 p.m., and said she was going out of town with Rita. I had introduced Rita to my wife a few months back, and they started being *"road dawgs."* But Rita was a freak that was cheating on her husband; so you know I didn't trust my wife with her. I didn't trust me with her.

Anyway, my wife left on a Friday and wouldn't answer her phone, call home to say she reached her destination, or nothing. I was like, *"Well damn! even I called home when I was creeping."*

It wasn't until Sunday, about 3:00 p.m. when the phone rang: *"Hello. How the kids doing?"* she asked. I said, *"You asking me about the damn kids. Where have you been? Why haven't you called?"*

Then my wife said, *"I didn't call to argue with you; put my children on the phone."*

I said, *"No! you gonna talk to me…"* Before I could say another word, she hung up on me.

I had already called her dad, and asked him to please keep his daughter at his house until I've calmed down. But he didn't heed my anger. I was so enraged by the amount of disrespect and carelessness that my wife displayed, when she walked through that door, that I could have murdered her on the spot. *I'm sorry, but that's how I felt at that time.*

She came there with her daughter, smiling like everything was okay. That alone infuriated me even more.

156

I asked her where she'd been, and why all this disrespect all of a sudden. But she just snickled and gave me an evil grin of reprisal…in a *"time to settle the score"* sarcasm.

My wife noticed I had her bags packed, down by the front door. She asked me in a mocking tone, *"Hmmm… Are these supposed to be my clothes? I know you are not calling yourself putting me out."*

I told her it was best for her to go until I've calmed down. But she must've thought I was joking because she forced herself by me, *"Boy, move out my way."* She walked up the steps, and I told her daughter to wait down stairs while I talked with her mother.

So here we are yelling and fussing with each other, my wife throwing shit up in my face from the past, out of spite, and used that as a means for her rebellion. But could I blame her? After all the things I have done to literally reduce her self-esteem to nothing, how can I blame her if she have reached that point. I couldn't. That's why it hurt so bad, to see her finally stand up to me and say *"Fuck you, Raw. Yes! I have a friend. And if I need somewhere to stay, you better believe I have somewhere to go."*

That hit the final nerve. She walked out of the room, and I stormed behind her with more of her bags. She screamed *"Put my shit down. I will have you leave up out of here before I do."*

I knew my wife have learned to be deceptive, but I didn't know she would go this far and have a plan up her sleeve that would hit me so hard that I thought I would never regain my composure.

We argued intensely outside of our bedroom, by the staircase…I yelled and screamed at the top of my lungs, *"So, you think you gonna cheat on me and brag about it to my face…Bitch, you probably sucked…"* But before I could get it out, she replied *"I tried to, but it couldn't fit in my mouth."*

"What?" That comment alone floored me and sent my pressure thru the roof. I couldn't take anymore of her blatant disrespect as she became transparent with her own confessions.

As she turned to walk down the steps, she kept inching by me saying *"You better not push me down these steps!"* As I tried to throw her things down the steps, she reached back and said *"Put my things down."* At that time I watched her "dramatically" slip down the steps, all the way to the bottom…pausing at a few steps as she went down.

When she reached the bottom, she claimed she hit her head on the wall and cracked her back. But it was amazing to see how fast she jumped up and said *"I got you now."*

I did not know what she meant when she said that. But she must've had it all planned out to provoke me to the point of violence.

No, I didn't ask her was she okay when she slipped because I was piping mad, and my anger made me care less if she sprained or broke anything during her fake "motion-picture" fall. When she said "I got you," I had no idea she had ran into the living room to call "911." I thought she would at least call her dad or her brothers. But no, she had called the police and was on the phone until they arrived.

I knew that they would've probably asked me to leave the house, until my anger subsided. But I had no idea that she was on the phone telling them that I was threatening to kill her and the children with a gun.

I was in the kitchen when the police rang the doorbell. Her daughter had answered the door, while my wife was still on the phone with 911. I heard the police whisper to her daughter, *"Where is he?"*

At the same time, I heard my wife say, *"Thank you. They are here."* At that point I walked towards the door and told the police it wasn't that serious to be waving guns. When I got to the door, I noticed police all around my house and more was pulling up. But I still didn't know that she had mentioned anything about guns. Not until the police asked, "Do you have any weapons on you?" *"Weapons?"* I asked confusingly. *"Can you step outside, please?"* The officer said.

When I stepped outside, they automatically threw me up against the house and handcuffed me. I was like *"Damn. We had a simple misunderstanding."* But the cops totally shocked me when they asked my wife to come to the door.

"Don't worry ma'am, we have him apprehended." The officer said.

All of a sudden my wife came by the door, sobbing and said *"Thank you, officers. He was threatening to shoot me…He said he was going to kill me."*

I was like, *"Huh? What is she talking about?"*

The police asked *"Do you know where his guns are?"* I was like "What guns?"

The police screamed at me, and said *"Be quiet. You are in enough trouble."*

I witnessed my wife putting on a serious acting role as if she was the battered housewife and I was the crazed lunatic.

I couldn't believe my eyes and I couldn't believe my ears. But sure enough, she escorted two officers upstairs and they came down with a handgun and a clip that I've never seen before, and said *"We got him."*

I looked to the sky and my heart cried *"God, I know my life is not going to end like this."*

I was hauled off to Richmond City Lock up, and charged with attempted murder and felony gun possession. I can get up to twenty five years....The Magistrate denied my bond...and the following day, the Judge did too.

CONFESSION 33

A SOLUTION TO AN UNHAPPY MARRIAGE: MAYBE I DESERVED TO LOSE YOU.

To My wife,

This is an apology, for the lies and the pain you had to endure over the years. I tried to shift the blame, but it wasn't you...It was me!

It was my fault and I'm sorry for cheating on you. I should have acted more responsibly loving you. I was so inconsiderate of your feelings and I apologize for neglecting you.

Please forgive me. I was wrong to share with another woman what should have been exclusively yours. You were right and I was wrong. My thoughtlessness has upset your heart, and that is inexcusable. I knew better, yet my actions proved how thoughtless I could be and I messed up again. I'm definitely the blame for a lot of mishaps in your life and I would like to make amends.

I cannot change what I did, but I hope that you can find it in your heart to forgive me. So that you can move on, have a happy life beyond me, and not hold a grudge in your heart. You had put your heart and soul into our marriage, and I totally took it all for granted. Sometimes the only solution to an unhappy marriage is a divorce.
It took a lot of courage, but you were right to leave me.

Maybe I Deserved that,
Raw

CONFESSION 34:
THE DAY I MET "KARMA"

2 weeks later, after the arrest......

I was in my cell, on my bunk reading when I heard the Deputy call my last name for a special visit. The first thought in mind was "Thank God, I hope it's my attorney with a date set for bail." So I hurriedly put on my state issued slacks and button up, then slipped on my shoes as I heard the Deputy yell out "Open cell 11." When I arrived at the visiting room, to my surprise it was not my attorney but my wife. It was so good to see her, and I didn't even think about the fact that she had me locked up on some bogus charges. I was just happy to see her smiling, coming to see her husband and being by my side during this ordeal.

"Hey, baby." I said.

"Hey, Raw. How you doing in here?" she said sarcastically.

"It's never a good place to be but I'm holding my head." I replied.

Then I seen her dig into her handbag, pulled out a folder with some papers that she was getting ready to hand over to me.

"I'm glad for you. I need you with a clear head." She said as she handed me the papers. "I would like a divorce." She said confidently.

"Baby, what are you talking about a divorce?" I asked in a sad tone.

"Please, don't make this harder than it already is...just sign the papers."
 She edged me on to quiet down and sign the divorce papers on her terms.

"How can you do this to me, like this? You're my wife." I said.
"Oh, really...Now, I'm your wife? Boy, you funny. She said mockingly.
"Just sign the damn papers!"

It was very shocking to me that my wife had become a woman I no longer knew. It was like she had this black cloud removed from her, and she had a glow like....like she was in love.

"Baby, I don't wanna lose my wife...What is happening to you?" I asked empathically.

"You happened to me. You...you...you! She started pointing and crying. So, sign the divorce papers and I can be done with you."

"Baby, I can't sign no papers like this...We need to talk. I need to be out of this predicament so we can talk, baby." I said pleadingly.

"Stop calling me baby...I am no longer your baby." She said wiping her eyes.

Soon as she said that, the visit door opened, and I seen my mechanic walked in. I thought "Wow, even my mechanic is showing me love on a visit." But he wasn't there for me. He walked over, hugged and kissed my wife.

"Baby, you okay; you ready?" He said to my wife, while passing her tissues to wipe her eyes.
I was shocked and angry at the same time as I hit the window and started going off.

"Yo, Kevin, what the hell are you doing with my wife...Dude? Dude, you played me...." I started screaming and hitting the window.

"Yo, they set me up...Yo, they set me up!" I started screaming as the guards rushed in and grabbed and subdued me because of all the commotion I was causing. All I heard was my wife saying to the Deputy, "Don't forget to tell him to sign the divorce papers."

When I got back to my cell, I had other mail and papers waiting for me... a separation order, a restraining order and divorce papers. This was the day I met "Karma."

(to be continued...)

DON'T JUDGE ME, PRAY FOR ME.

THIS IS MY CONFESSION...

"IF TOMORROW NEVER COMES"

"TELL MY BABY MOTHER, IT WASN'T MY INTENTIONS TO HURT HER...
I HOPE SHE FIND SOMEONE WHO DESERVES HER;
I HOPE THERE'S NO HARD FEELINGS....
IF I COULD REWRITE ONE SENTENCE OF MY LIFE,
I WOULD WRITE THE WORDS I NEVER SAID,
TELL YOU I LOVED YOU FOR EVERY SINGLE DAY....
IF I COULD SOMEHOW TURN BACK THE HANDS OF TIME,
I WOULDN'T WASTE A MOMENT ARGUING,
AND I'LL NEVER PUT YOU THROUGH THAT SH*T AGAIN......
CAUSE IF TOMORO NEVER COMES, AND YOU NEVER SEE ME AGAIN...
I DON'T WANT YOUR LAST MEMORY OF ME, TO BE FILLED WITH ALL
THAT NEGATIVITY....
SEE, ALL THAT FUSSIN 'N FIGHTING WON'T MEAN NOTHING,
WHEN IT'S ALL SAID AND DONE.......
IF TOMORROW NEVER COMES......"

LYRICS & SONG BY
LYFE JENNINGS

COMING SOON TO A CITY NEAR YOU:

"LOVE, LIES N CONSEQUENCES"

THE HIT STAGEPLAY

CHECK FOR TOUR SCHEDULE AT

WWW.LOVELIESCONSEQUENCES.COM

ORDER THIS BOOK AND OTHERS BY THIS
AUTHOR AT:
  AMAZON.COM AND KINDLE.

GOOGLE INFO: **RAW, THE CHEATOLOGIST**

PUBLISHER: **BABYDADDY PUBLISHING**

EMAIL:
THECHEATOLOGIST@GMAIL.COM

YOUTUBE SEARCH: THE CHEATOLOGIST

WEBSITE:
WWW.LOVELIESCONSEQUENCES.COM

FACEBOOK**: THECHEATOLOGIST**

TWITTER: **THE CHEATOLOGIST**

INSTAGRAM: **THECHEATOLOGIST**

LINKEDIN: **THECHEATOLOGIST**

FOR BOOK CLUB MEETINGS, SPEAKING, ETC...
EMAIL REQUEST:
THECHEATOLOGIST@GMAIL.COM

www.ingramcontent.com/pod-product-compliance
Lightning Source LLC
Chambersburg PA
CBHW072011290326
41934CB00007BA/1008